TAILS

from the

AFTERLIFE

To Write to the Author

If you wish to contact the author or would like more information about this book, please write to the author in care of Llewellyn Worldwide Ltd. and we will forward your request. Both the author and publisher appreciate hearing from you and learning of your enjoyment of this book and how it has helped you. Llewellyn Worldwide Ltd. cannot guarantee that every letter written to the author can be answered, but all will be forwarded. Please write to:

Kristy Robinett
℅ Llewellyn Worldwide
2143 Wooddale Drive
Woodbury, MN 55125-2989

Please enclose a self-addressed stamped envelope for reply, or $1.00 to cover costs. If outside the U.S.A., enclose an international postal reply coupon.

Many of Llewellyn's authors have websites with additional information and resources. For more information, please visit our website at http://www.llewellyn.com.

TAILS

from the

AFTERLIFE

STORIES OF SIGNS, MESSAGES & INSPIRATION
FROM YOUR ANIMAL COMPANIONS

KRISTY ROBINETT

Llewellyn Publications
Woodbury, Minnesota

FIRST EDITION
First Printing, 2018

Cover design by Kevin R. Brown

Llewellyn Publications is a registered trademark of Llewellyn Worldwide Ltd.

Library of Congress Cataloging-in-Publication Data (Pending)
ISBN: 978-0-7387-5217-4

Llewellyn Worldwide Ltd. does not participate in, endorse, or have any authority or responsibility concerning private business transactions between our authors and the public.

All mail addressed to the author is forwarded but the publisher cannot, unless specifically instructed by the author, give out an address or phone number.

Any Internet references contained in this work are current at publication time, but the publisher cannot guarantee that a specific location will continue to be maintained. Please refer to the publisher's website for links to authors' websites and other sources.

Llewellyn Publications
A Division of Llewellyn Worldwide Ltd.
2143 Wooddale Drive
Woodbury, MN 55125-2989
www.llewellyn.com

Printed in the United States of America

Other Books by Kristy Robinett

It's a Wonderful Afterlife

Messages From a Wonderful Afterlife

Messenger Between Worlds

Journey to the Afterlife

DEDICATION

To all the fur babies I've loved but am assured I'll see again. Until then, play and run, and keep visiting. My heart will always wear the paw prints left by you.

Acknowledgments

This book could not have happened without the hundreds of thousands of clients and their loved ones on the Other Side who have touched my life more than I could ever eloquently communicate. I'm so grateful for being a messenger and helping to make the connections.

My gratitude goes out to Llewellyn Publishing, especially Amy Glaser, who inspires me daily to reach for my dreams, and to Stephanie Finne and the rest of the hardworking staff.

I am thankful to my own spirit guides for teaching me that learning and exploring never gets old, and that it doesn't necessarily have to take place in a classroom.

To my husband, Chuck Robinett, for his constant support and unconditional love. My children, Micaela Even Kempf, Connor Even, Cora Kutnick, and Molly Robinett, who (I think) I haven't embarrassed too much. To my dad, who's my biggest pain and my largest love. My mom-in-law, Mary Lou, who always has a story to tell, a hug to share, and wisdom to give. To my dad, Ron, for his newly developed patience and understanding.

Love to my brother, Duane Schiller, and sister, Cheri Ford, for dad-sitting and listening to me complain and whine.

I am thankful for having some of the best friends ever, especially Mikey and Marjanna McClain, our travel buddies, who so lovingly help us with events and late-night laughs.

Mary Byberg, my assistant and friend, who's always kind and patient with my clients and most of all with me.

My best friends and confidantes, Gayle Buchan, Donna Shorkey, and Jenni Licata. Thank you to Colleen Kwiecinski and her mad Cooper-sitting skills. Courtney Sierra for being the best hair counselor around. To Jan Tomes, Kathy Curatolo, and Ryan Sparks for their friendship and help with events. SUP. To Dr. David Schindler, Nancy Schindler, Deneen Baxter, and so many others—without you I wouldn't continue my dream.

Finally, to my furry loves who offer unconditional love and cuddles, Gracie May, Archibald, Lucy Lou, Jinxie Jean, Isabella, Raven Lee, and Cooper. I will forever love you as you get old and gray, and even into the afterlife.

CONTENTS

DISCLAIMER

Although the stories are based on real-life occurrence, some names and identifying details have been changed to protect the privacy of individuals.

INTRODUCTION

I've never been fond of the word *death*. Death means the end of life, and that every memory, obstacle, love, and lesson was for naught and deemed meaningless. At three years of age, I was seeing spirits, which was proof to me that death didn't exist except for what happened to the physical body. It's that physical absence that creates the deep void of sadness, including the loss of a loved one that might have a cold nose, whiskers, and a wagging tail.

I always envisioned a pet psychic being like the fictional character Doctor Dolittle, a veterinarian who understands what the animals are saying, only add in a telepathy aspect. It wasn't until several years ago that I had an *aha* moment and realized that each one of us can be an animal communicator if we want to be. It's not that animal communicators have an automatic built-in animal translator; we just have to have the patience to learn their language.

With animals we have to pick up on the subtle and sometimes not so subtle cues. Maybe that is why there are people who don't like animals; they lack the patience or instinct. With humans we rely on verbal communication, and while animals have their own verbal communication they also convey their thoughts emotionally, through body language, and through scent. The cat that rubs up against your leg. The dog that wags its tail. The hedgehog that rolls up and hides. The skunk that sprays. The twitch of an eyebrow. The snarl of the mouth. Humans think and speak of the past, present, and future, real and imagined. Animals rely on current and present stimuli. Humans learn how to communicate, while animals communicate instinctively and follow through intuitively.

When we transition over to the Other Side, we have to learn how to communicate differently. Without vocal chords, we learn a universal language. Some spirits call it the language of love, and not everyone here in the earthly realm knows how to resonate on that level. Animals vibrate at a similar frequency on the Other Side as they do here, and so the language is similar.

I've discussed in my previous books *It's a Wonderful Afterlife* and *Messages from a Wonderful Afterlife* the steps it takes for a human to cross over, something I've classified as the Heaven Chronicles. Several poems and legends use the term *Rainbow Bridge* for when a pet passes on and crosses over.

The Rainbow Bridge legends say that once a pet's physical body passes, the animal is restored back to its perfect self—healthy and whole. The pet waits in a beautiful meadow where it spends its time playing. Once the owner passes, the owner and beloved pet meet up once again at the Rainbow Bridge. Then, they cross into Heaven, side by side, together and never again to be separated. Not to take away the beautiful imagery, but the Other Side has explained animal crossings a bit differently to me.

THE HEAVEN CHRONICLES FOR HUMAN SOULS

First, let me explain what happens when a human soul crosses over.

The Cross Over

Once the physical body dies, the soul and spirit leave the body to take the journey to the Other Side. Some have described it as a long tunnel, others as a stairwell, and yet others as a doorway. Just as we have free will and free choice here on Earth, the free will continues to step into the unknown of the light.

The Soul Review

A soul review, or life review, occurs after we cross over. This involves watching your life and all those you've encountered and impacted, all the actions you've done—the good and the bad. It is a teaching tool to understand that life, and death, is to be lived consciously.

Angel Boot Camp

After the soul review, you get to make the decisions as to what is next. Some choose to quickly reincarnate and others decide to take time to reflect. Some decide to do what is called a soul split, which is leaving a piece of the soul in Heaven and incarnate another piece. Those who decide to stick around, choose what their Heaven is and who it includes, as long as it coincides with the other soul.

There aren't any clocks or time on the Other Side, but from an earthly plane explanation, this step takes six to twelve months. That is why I urge those seeking an appointment with any medium to wait at least six months, but preferably twelve months, so that their loved ones are unpacked, settled, and have found their voice once more. After all, without a physical body, we don't have vocal chords to talk, right?

We are also given an opportunity to help others. This may come in the means of being someone's spirit guide or a loved one's guardian. It could also be an occupation in Heaven, but whatever it is, it's something you choose and you will love. You won't ever get that "do I really have to get up in the morning?" feeling here.

Living in Heaven

If a soul hasn't reincarnated, then this is when living occurs—really living. You spend time with those you want to spend time with and do what makes you the most happy, with so much joy. Heaven exists all around the living. It isn't a place like we think of in the earthly sense.

CREATURES BIG AND SMALL

The Latin roots of the word *animal*, *anima* and *animus*, mean "soul" or "spirit." *Anima*, the feminine form, has the root meaning "breath, air, life force," while the masculine form, *animus*, has the root meaning "mind or intellect." Secondary meanings are "passion" and "spirited." It's no wonder that animals have such a special connection to us, whether it is the beautiful cardinal on the snow-covered pine tree or a pet beagle that playfully runs around with a tennis ball. Is it that they are with life force or that they give us life force?

The Tibetans believed that the souls of humans and animals can reincarnate into any living form, including into a simple worm. Although maybe a bit extreme, modern Tibetans do believe that compassion and love should be shown to every living thing, no matter the size, stature, or status. Humans have an ego that categorizes who is the highest of the evolutionary ladder of life, nature does not.

Ancient Greek philosophers believed in metempsychosis, the soul reincarnation from human form to animal form. The concept can be mind-boggling to think of what happens to every single living thing. Was Uncle Fred a flea in a past life? Or maybe a dinosaur? Does every single bird that passes away go to Heaven? Is there enough room? You can drive yourself mad thinking about it. Many who study the metaphysical grasp the concept by what is referred to as group consciousness, meaning that certain species of different animal souls combine into one soul. This is especially true for animals in nature. Domesticated animals are given an identity by their humans and therefore don't group. They are gifted an identity, therefore a soul and a spirit, which enable them to have a place on the Other Side.

THE HEAVEN CHRONICLES FOR ANIMAL SOULS

There are differences between how the human soul and the animal soul transition to the Other Side, although the differences are not drastic.

The Cross Over

Once the physical body dies, it is released from pain and injury. Animals don't fear death or what is yet to come. They travel into the light and journey to the Other Side. There is no soul review or angel boot camp. Animals, although known to carry memories and grudges, aren't as complicated as human beings. They are much more forgiving, and thus they don't need the teaching tools that humans need.

The Meet Up

They are then greeted by their human. If their human isn't on the Other Side, a soul that is attached to their human cares for the animal until their human makes their journey and a reunion takes place.

Living in Heaven

They are surrounded by support, love, and comfort, playing and relaxing with other animal souls.

IT HURTS

Animals come in all shapes and sizes. They come into our lives in all different ways, but their love is tried, true, and unconditional. Losing a beloved pet is horrible. I've witnessed as many tears shed over a lost animal friend as I have the loss of a human family member, which speaks volumes to the unconditional love that our pets offer. Our pets comfort us during sadness and sickness. They snuggle and sleep with us. Their loyalty is unfathomable and their judgments obsolete. If you're late coming home from work, there's no argument over where you've been, just simple happiness that you're home. Even if they pout, they don't hold grudges, at least for long, especially if you give them a treat. They play with us and exercise us, and they constantly remind us that life is too short to not have fun. Yet they don't live forever, unfortunately. In fact, most don't live long enough at all.

I've never once claimed to be an animal psychic. I am a psychic medium who happens to be an animal lover. I communicate with the Other Side and have since I was just a toddler, my first experience when I was told by a spirit that my grandmother was going to die. After informing my mom of the news, I was met by a swat on the backside. It was soon after my prediction that my grandma unexpectedly passed away. That wasn't the only spirit that I was seeing, hearing, and talking to—there were many others, and they soon became labeled as my imaginary friends by my family. It was harmless. It wasn't as if I caused my grandmother's passing, but it spooked my parents nonetheless. Hoping to keep me busy, and away from all of the so-called imaginary friends or dead people, my mom and dad registered me at the local Lutheran school a year earlier than I technically should have started.

Anytime I attempted to talk to my mom about what I was experiencing, she would roll her eyes and tell me to just stop. It wasn't that she was coldhearted or uncaring; I now understand that she just didn't know how to help me. Her means of dealing with my unknown world was ignoring it and hoping for it to go away or for me to outgrow it. The spirits didn't go away, and instead of outgrowing it I grew into it, but I learned to just not talk about it much, if at all.

I was gifted with all the clairs, although that sounds like an illness. And to be perfectly honest, for a long time I thought it was. What it means is I'm able to receive messages by seeing an energy in their physical and earthly form in both the physical and sometimes in the mind's eye. I also have the ability to feel energy and pick up on the emotional, mental, and physical pain. I have the ability to acquire information by hearing, I'm able to smell and taste from the ethereal realms, and I'm able to know details of information with a psychic knowing.

I don't believe that I have superpowers or that I'm special. I believe everybody has the opportunity to access these abilities—one, some, or all—if they want to. It is through recognizing the different gifts that you can access your loved ones, pets included, on the Other Side.

I've spent a lot of time wondering why, after all the obstacles (namely my parents and Lutheran schooling), I was able to continue to access the clairs. It was a visit with my Lutheran Missouri Synod minister that helped put it into perspective.

I'd gone through a terrible divorce (which I know the majority of divorces are), when the psychic and medium abilities were becoming hard to control and even harder to understand. So I did three things to help explain and/or extradite it. I saw a therapist, who told me that I was experiencing psychic abilities and handed me some books to read. I saw a neurologist, who did every test under the sun and, with normal test results in hand, told me that I was experiencing mediumistic abilities. And I saw my minister, who, after my confessional of sorts, I ended up giving a reading to. It was the minister who handed me a business card of a metaphysical center and told me to talk to them. I was lucky in that I was put on the path of the right people at the right time. The metaphysical center became a spot for a group of misfit Lutherans, including a retired Lutheran minister, who were experiencing collective clairs. It was there that I began to do official readings and consultations with clients. It was there that I found a sense of belonging. And even fifteen plus years later, I am still the first to admit that what I experience is strange and weird, filled with constant unknowns and more questions than answers.

It's often those who've had their own psychic or paranormal experiences who begin to explore the realm of the unknown, wanting to believe, some needing to believe, and having the reassurance that there is an afterlife. When it is a beloved pet, there is no difference.

There are many losses that we grieve, but a pet is one of the worst. Even if it might've been their time to go, that doesn't stop the heart from hurting and missing them. You'll meet them in the light, on the Other Side, and although their physical body is gone, they aren't gone. Whisper their names, take a moment to tune in, because Heaven does have visiting hours and it is filled with wet noses, wagging tails, and lots of love that they still share in spirit from the Other Side.

GHOSTS, LEGENDS
& TOTEMS

Accounts of animal ghosts have existed for a very long time. Legends of mysterious animals appearing in the middle of the road and simply disappearing and tales of experiencing—seeing, feeling, or hearing—a beloved pet that has moved on from this earthly realm.

There is a difference between a ghost and a spirit, though. This is a common mix up. A ghost is a soul that has decided to not move on to the Other Side. While a spirit has already made its transition and is simply visiting from the Other Side, sometimes continuing its normal routine of jumping on the bed, nudging an owner's hand, moving the empty food dish, or playing with its living furry friends.

Several years back my husband and I went to Gettysburg, Pennsylvania. I have an uncanny ability to plan trips to notoriously haunted locations for our wedding anniversary, and this was one of them. It was a quiet October weekend and the typical bustling streets of town were eerily empty. Even more eerie was that the battlefields that are typically filled with reenactment actors instead sat desolate. With the cold, and even a few snowflakes flurrying, dusk sat on the horizon for what felt like half the day. The battlefields close at 10 p.m. in the autumn and it was already almost 9 p.m., so we headed out by Seminary Ridge. The area of open terrain was dark except for our headlights. We were instructed by a guide to sit on the side of the road, windows down, lights off, and just listen.

"You'll hear the gunshots," he told us. "You'll hear the cries."

Chuck hadn't yet turned off the headlights when we saw a shadow coming toward us. We recognized it as what looked to be a soldier on horseback.

"Probably a ranger checking to see who's still in the park," I said.

Chuck nodded in agreement, but when we looked again, the shadow was gone. No horse. No soldier. No anybody. Now plain curious, Chuck started the car and slowly inched along the road, both of us looking left and right, but there wasn't a soul to be seen.

That morning over breakfast, the other lodgers shared their stories with the innkeeper, and then we shared ours.

"We call him the watcher," the innkeeper said. "Not sure who he is exactly, but he often appears on rainy nights. Just last week a group of ten saw him around that same area. They said he had a dog with him, too."

"We didn't see a dog," I said. "Any idea who the dog is?"

"That would be Sallie," the innkeeper told us.

Sallie Ann Jarrett was the canine mascot of the 11th Pennsylvania Infantry. She was a pit bull terrier that was a gift to Captain William R. Terry of Company I in May 1861. She was a smart pup, and she joined the soldiers for their drills, marching twice with

President Abraham Lincoln. She fought in several battles, including Bull Run and Fredericksburg. She accompanied Captain Terry throughout most all of the Civil War, until she was killed in action.

On July 1, 1863, in Gettysburg, she was separated from the regiment at Cemetery Hill. The soldiers feared she was killed, but she was instead guarding her wounded men at Oak Ridge. It was February 6, 1865, during the Union advance at Hatcher's Run, Virginia, when she was struck by a bullet and killed. Although the battle continued, the soldiers gave her a burial, but it is in Gettysburg where a life-size bronze statue of Sallie is.

"Legend says she still watches over her wounded and dead."

We had seen her statue, but we were completely unaware of her significance.

The irony wasn't lost on us that the dog ghost shared the same name as my mother, who passed in 2006. I often speak of Heaven hellos and although we didn't see Sallie, we both felt as if it was my mom letting us know she was around, watching over us too.

GHOSTS AND THEIR PETS

The South loves their porches, and they love their animals, too. Nestled in a neighborhood in Charleston, South Carolina, is a grand Victorian home. Built in 1888, the grand mansion now serves as a restaurant named after the pup that once called it home, and some believe still does.

It is said that when the owners sold the home they left their little dog, Poogan, to fend for himself. Poogan became a fixture in the neighborhood, wandering from porch to porch, looking for love and scraps. Nobody much minded—everyone loved Poogan—and he became the official greeter when the restaurant opened in 1976.

Poogan died a natural death in 1979 at the age of nine years old and is buried on the property; a small gravestone and statue marks his grave. The restaurant, and the porch, is named in his honor.

Many, however, have seen Poogan napping on the porch, alive and well. They even say they've pet and fed him, and they are shocked when they are told there is no little dog and they've just encountered Poogan's spirit.

One night several years ago, my husband and I made an impromptu trip to Charleston with a ghost tour. We stopped in front of Poogan's, where his grave marker was pointed out and the spot where he would often nap.

"Can I take a photo?" a tourist asked our guide.

The guide smiled and nodded and the lady took several pictures around the grand house. As we walked she scrolled through the photos and stopped. "Look," she said, showing the guide. "Look, what is that?"

One photo she'd taken of Poogan's had a glow of a bright blue light at the same spot Poogan is often seen. "We have to go back and look," the guide said.

And we did. There was nothing to cause the blue light, and no matter how we tried to debunk it we just couldn't. No other photo before or after that one showed anything unusual. I often say sometimes you have to just take it for what it is—Poogan greeting us like he did forty years before.

CATS AND THE SUPERNATURAL

Edgar Allan Poe is a name notorious for gothic horror, but Poe loved animals, especially cats. Stopping at the ornate gates of a local cemetery, the Charleston guide began the story of Poe's famous Annabelle Lee. Right above us on the rooftop sat a cat, paws crossed, listening intently. As the guide wrapped up the story, the cat climbed down into the cemetery before squeezing between the gates and joining the group, sitting just a few feet from Chuck and me.

The tour guide walked slowly to us, the cat unmoving. "You know I tell this story every night, and every single night during the same story a cat joins in. I've been doing this tour for years. It isn't always the same cat, but a cat nonetheless. I have always wondered if it was perhaps … you'll think this is crazy," she laughed.

"Honestly, I won't think it's crazy," I answered, thinking that if I told her what I did for a living she might find it cool or kooky.

"Do you think the cat is Poe? I don't know why I never think it is Annabel, but I don't. Do you think it's Poe?" she asked again.

The history of cats is much more complex than dogs, which says a lot about the complexities of cats in general. Once believed to be conduits to the gods, cats were mummified with their owners in Egypt. In China and Japan, they believe that cats are luck and ward off bad spirits. In Europe, the cat helped contain dangerous diseases by hunting and killing dirty rodents, but also believed that cats held supernatural powers and could reanimate like a vampire. Because of the aloofness and mysteriousness of a cat, it was thought they also had the ability to sense auras and read minds, heal and destroy. Within literature and movies, cats were written as familiars, helping to conjure up the dead and create chaos among the living.

I didn't believe that Poe was the reincarnated cat, but I believed his spirit visited within the cat. Poe loved animals and even had his own cat, with his wife Virginia, that he doted on, believed to be a tortoise shell named Catterina. It would be just like him to love the attention and the supernatural, moodiness, and complexities of a cat.

LOYALTY IN LIFE AND AFTERLIFE

Right out of college, Mia accepted the job at her current company because it offered her the chance to travel the world. She was excited when her friend from school, Howie, was also recruited. The two had met at their university on the first day at freshman orientation and became fast friends. First days are always filled with excitement and high hopes, and lots of groups, fraternities, and sororities pitch their clubs and one of those was a paranormal team. As most kids grunted and laughed, Mia and Howie shared their own ghostly experiences and decided to join the paranormal group together. Unfortunately, a tough school load got in the way, and most everything took a backseat to their studies, sometimes even their friendship. There are some people who you don't have to talk to every day and it doesn't damage the friendship. Mia and Howie had that kind of relationship.

"I heard you were chosen to set up the office in Tokyo," Howie congratulated Mia.

Mia smiled wide and nodded.

"Guess who's coming with you?"

Mia squealed. Although unprofessional, she was excited, but nervous too. Having Howie there with her was icing on the cake. Her family was proud of her, but they weren't thrilled with her wanderlust. She kept telling them it was just a half year and she'd be back the week before Christmas.

After twenty-two hours and two layovers, Mia and Howie safely landed on a spring Thursday afternoon and found their way to their temporary home. Both night owls, after getting settled they decided to forage for food and see about some sightseeing excursions as they didn't have to start until Monday.

"We should ghost hunt," Howie suggested. "Like old times."

It was a dark moon when Mia and Howie wandered by the cemetery Aoyama Reien.

"Aw, look," Mia pointed at the small dog sitting by the entrance. A man wearing a plaid suit coat and dark slacks stood next to him.

"Can I pet him?" Mia asked the man, who smiled an agreement.

"Don't get any ideas on getting a pet," Howie warned.

Just as Mia reached out to pet the small dog's head, the man and the dog vanished in front of them. Howie and Mia both stared at one another in astonishment. A van pulled up with a ghost logo on it. A man guided tourists toward the cemetery entrance.

"Some of you may have heard of the story of Hachiko, most loyal of dogs. He is buried here. Some have even seen him with his owner, finally together."

Mia and Howie knew then who they'd seen.

Eizaburo Ueno was a professor at Tokyo University and was on the lookout for the perfect puppy when a student found him a purebred Japanese Akita dog. Ueno named the dog Hachiko, or Hachi, which became his nickname. Hachi wasn't just a dog to Ueno; he was his son, and they were inseparable.

Every morning, Hachi would walk Ueno to the Shibuya Train Station, in central Tokyo, to see him off to work. He would then meet him back at the station in the afternoon to walk him home. It was only two years after Ueno and Hachiko became a pair when his owner didn't show up. On May 21, 1925, Eiazburo suffered a cerebral hemorrhage and died suddenly while at work.

Hachiko was taken in by a family friend, but he spent the rest of his ten years faithfully walking to Shibuya Train Station every morning and afternoon, waiting for the return of his owner.

A newspaper picked up his story, which perpetuated his celebrity status, and people would visit him with treats and love. Hachiko, however, passed away peacefully and alone on the street near Shibuya Train Station on March 8, 1935, at twelve years old.

There are several monuments of the faithful dog, including at the train station and his original owner's gravesite; they stand as reminders of loyalty on Earth until the afterlife. Hachiko's grave is one of the most visited, and many leave behind candies, flowers, coins, dog toys, and other trinkets. Some people, like Mia and Howie, have even seen their spirits finally together.

Mia and Howie were engaged to get married by the time they returned to the States. Right after signing the papers for their new home, they rescued a puppy that they named Iko, after the legendary and loyal pup, and one of their most intriguing paranormal encounters.

TOMMY

Maria Lochi was an animal lover, and you'd often find her rescuing and caring for stray dogs. It was during one of her pet missions that Maria found Tommy, a German shepherd mix, abandoned in a field. Maria took Tommy in, and they immediately bonded. It was rare for Tommy to leave Maria's side, even attending church services with his owner. When Maria passed away, Tommy followed her coffin into the church for her funeral service. The mourners understood the deep connection and allowed him to stay.

Tommy was welcomed by the priests at the church of Santa Maria Assunta in the town of San Donaci, Italy. After the loss of his owner, he began to attend every mass, baptism, wedding, and funeral, running in just as the bells rang alerting the beginning of the service. Many believed he'd hope to see his owner. Others believed it was to show his devotion and dedication. Locals wanted to adopt Tommy but, although Maria's son took him in, Tommy was everyone's dog. He would often wander around the town visiting, but most times he could be found in the church where the cleric would leave the doors open just for him.

Many believed that Tommy saw the spirit of his owner and would sit near the spot that Maria always sat, looking up wistfully. It was just a few months after Maria's passing when Tommy passed away. Although he had many ailments, it was believed that he really passed from a broken heart.

Cynics may say Tommy simply created a routine and it had nothing to do with emotion or love, but then they probably never allowed themselves to experience the unconditional love of an animal. They ask for nothing other than a bit of food and companionship, yet they give so much more in return.

THE WHITE HOUSE

It's not a secret how many animals have made the White House their home, as the "first" pets have been known to make the headlines as much as the president's children. It's also no secret the many rumors that have circulated since the 1800s of the White House being haunted.

Half a dozen presidents and just as many first ladies have had paranormal encounters with translucent figures and eerie encounters. Abraham Lincoln and his wife held séances in hopes of communicating with their son Willy. Nancy Reagan held spirit circles as well.

The ghost of Dolley Madison, wife of James Madison, is said to appear in the Rose Garden, tending to her flowers that she proudly planted. Abigail Adams's spirit is said to be hanging laundry in the

East Room. Afterward, a faint smell of laundry detergent wafts through the air.

Lincoln dreamed of his own assassination three days before it actually happened, telling his wife and confidantes that he saw himself in a casket, surrounded by flowers. Since then, many presidents, family members, staff, and even visitors have seen the spirit of Lincoln guarding the Oval Office, while others said they've sensed his presence.

Many presidents bring their pets with them when they take office, many witnessing their animals acting out of sorts—staring, barking, growling, and even snarling at the corners of the rooms with nobody there to get that type of reaction. Animals are intuitive by nature, and they are thought to see and hear beyond what humans do, even into the afterlife.

President Reagan's Cavalier King Charles spaniel, Rex, was quite perceptive to the paranormal and would often bark when he was near the Lincoln Bedroom. One time, Rex stood up on his hind legs, pointed his nose at the ceiling, and barked frantically, which was not typical behavior for the normally calm dog.

Abraham Lincoln had a soft heart and loved animals. When he was elected president, he left his dog back home because of Fido's fear for loud noises, but he couldn't possibly live without animals. He became the first president who added cats to the White House by bringing in two kittens, Tabby and Dixie. Lincoln instantly grew attached to the felines, and it is reported that he would feed the cats at the table with a golden fork, to the horror of his wife. The staff joked that Lincoln's hobby was rescuing cats, so it was no surprise that during a winter visit to the battlefield he found several half-frozen kittens and simply tucked them in his coat and brought them back home. It was soon after Lincoln's presidency when there became reports of DC.

Referred to as the Demon Cat, or DC, this cute and cuddly black cat is often discovered lurking in the White House basement, along with multiple other government buildings. At first it appears harmless, a stray, many believe, but once approached it grows in size and lunges before disappearing in thin air. Supposedly, the ghost cat's main home is the basement crypt in the Capitol, originally planned to be the final resting place of George Washington. At one time, the Capitol was infested with rats and, in order to remedy the problem, caretakers released a large number of cats to control the rat population. This cat, however, may be chasing rats, but not of the rodent kind. DC is said to primarily show up before tragedies and was first seen in March 1865 and then again the day before Lincoln was assassinated. DC was again seen a couple days before Kennedy was killed.

DC came up during a reading I had with Meryl. I had read for Meryl for years. She would often come in for a session when visiting her family in Michigan, but her home for two decades was Maryland, where she worked as a government employee in Washington, DC. She had just lost a family pet and was curious if they truly went to Heaven.

"Sure," I told her. "Why would something we love be stolen from us forever?"

"I know you do those ghost tours and deal with spooky stuff. Can I tell you something I've never been able to wrap my head around, which is why I'm confused?"

Of course I was intrigued.

"It was September 7, 2001, the Friday before September 11, when I had to go into the basement of one of the buildings to get a file." Meryl pursed her lips together before continuing. "As soon as I swiped my access card and opened the door to the office, I felt the energy shift, and then I saw it. I saw the shadow. It was a dark shadow and then it transformed into what looked like a black panther. I couldn't move. I couldn't scream. I thought for certain I was dead. It looked at me, turned around, and disappeared."

"And you've heard the rumors of DC?" I asked.

"Sure, but we thought they were simply a creepy legend, or someone who drank too much the night before," Meryl laughed before turning serious again. Pulling her phone out of her purse, she swiped to a picture and handed me the phone. On the screen was a black-and-white Old English sheepdog. Wiping a tear away, she took the phone back and continued, "This has me thinking, though, that maybe there wasn't a Heaven for animals. Maybe there isn't a Heaven for people."

"There's a Heaven," I assured her. "Back to DC, though. There's got to be cameras. Have they ever seen anything on the cameras?"

Meryl mischievously grinned and winked with knowing.

ANIMAL GUIDES

Animals are said to be very perceptive to the Other Side. They walk in an alpha state of being, that relaxed and meditated state that us humans have seemed to forget how to channel, at least on a natural basis. It is this alpha state that helps animals see through the veil of this world into the Other Side, and quite possibly the other way around, too. This helps them become a guide and a protector to animals and humans from Heaven. Each one of us has an animal guide or animal guides that are connected to us. Whether we want them or even know they are there, they are assigned to us to help guide us through our everyday life filled with decisions, celebrations, and heartaches. We often will have a dream with our animal guide in it, or simply have a special affinity for a particular type of animal. They protect us, educate us, and even heal us.

So is the White House DC a ghost, a demon, a shapeshifter, or overactive imagination, or maybe a Heaven helper? Through the Native American legends, werecats show up to protect humans, not hurt them. Many Native American tribes speak of man transforming from man to beast or animal to another animal. These shifters, sometimes called skinwalkers, are believed to be black in color, which is connected with its evil or poison. According to University of Nevada, Las Vegas, anthropologist Dan Benyshek, who specializes in the study of Native Americans of the Southwest, "Skinwalkers are purely evil in intent. I'm no expert on it, but the general view is that skinwalkers do all sorts of terrible things—they make people sick, they commit murders. They are grave robbers and necrophiliacs. They are greedy and evil people who must kill a sibling or other relative to be initiated as a skinwalker. They supposedly can turn into were-animals and can travel in supernatural ways."

Anthropologist David Zimmerman, of the Navajo Nation Historic Preservation Department, has a bit of a different take. "Skinwalkers are folks that possess knowledge of medicine, medicine both practical (heal the sick) and spiritual (maintain harmony), and they are both wrapped together in ways that are nearly impossible to untangle."

We may never know who or what the Demon Cat is, but I believe it helps to give a bit of a different perspective. It was the Native Americans who originally owned the land that the Capitol sits on, and the tribes to this day believe that we are all given different animal guides, also called spirit guides or sometimes called power animals. It is these animals that come in and out of our lives depending on the journey.

Native Americans believe that your spirit animal assists you throughout your life and afterlife, in the physical and spiritual world. There is a connection with your spirit animal that can come through dreams, signs, symbolisms, or other interactions.

This animal guide offers power and wisdom whether or not you know your animal guide. It is the lesson that is most valuable. We learn from animals, both domesticated and free, each having their own heritage of folklore and symbolism. Definitions may change slightly due to time, place, and culture, but due to the animal's characteristics, habitat, and position in the eco-system, the theme is often similar.

THE LEGENDS

In Native American culture, totems or animal guides are encountered through intention. Some come in a trance, meditation, or simply taking a journey in nature. They can be revealed in a physical form, in a vision or dream, or symbolically.

An animal guide helps you with your present life situation. Each spirit animal has its own skills and knowledge in order to assist you with whatever you are going through. Your animal guide is chosen for you and appears when you are in need of the wisdom. On the other hand, a totem animal is an animal spirit that is invoked, or called upon when facing a specific situation.

Australian aborigines would venture into a walkabout, where a man would break off from the daily grind and walk in solitude across the desert and bush country on a spiritual quest. These journeys would often cover 1,000 miles or more, and they were done without any equipment. During this journey, the walker allows him- or herself to be guided through a spiritual power, often with the help of their animal totem or animal guide. It was believed that before human existence, animals and plants existed with just a soul, not yet physical. When the time presented itself, all but one of the "souls" became plants or animals, with the last one becoming human and acting as a custodian or guardian to the natural world around them. It seemed that it continued that way into the afterlife.

They say that a dog is man's best friend. I've found that owls, goats, cats, ferrets, turtles, and every other animal can be as well. Animals have only basic needs. Their lives aren't contaminated with money, society, religion, pop culture, or the other garbage that moves humans away from simple connections. We may not all know our totem or our animal guide, but we walk beside them every day. Some we call our best friend and some are unknown, but they are there to help us get back to who we originally were, both in life and on the Other Side.

We are often aware that we have guardian angels, but we also have spirit animals that watch over us since birth, sometimes called a power animal or animal totem. You do not choose them, they choose you, just as you do when you get a pet. Often you intuitively will pick up on the type of animal without even realizing it. Animal totems may change throughout your lifetime, depending on your life situation.

Your spirit animal may not be so obvious, but you can identify what it is by simply asking your guides and guardians to have this animal appear in your dreams or in your waking time. It might not be that a hippopotamus knocks on your front door, but that you receive someone's social media status that mentions a joke with a hippo in it, and then you see a commercial with another hippo in it, and then a new billboard is put up with a hippo on it. There are no such things as coincidences in life. It's all synchronicities that shouldn't be discounted.

SLOTHS

Maggie came in for a session to talk about her job choices. She was almost done with her degree, but she was still unsure what she wanted to do. The first thing her guides showed me was sloths. I try not to discount even the oddest message, but this had me scratching my head. Maybe it meant she was going too slow or taking too long to think things through. Instead of ignoring the message, or interpreting it myself, I shared with her that I kept seeing sloths, which was met by a jaw drop.

"I know." I blushed. "Crazy!"

"No, you don't understand." She excitedly pulled her hair into a ponytail. "I was given an opportunity to work at a sloth sanctuary, and my parents think that I'm nuts for even considering it. This just validates that it's what I'm supposed to do."

"Sloths," I said out loud. "I've never seen this one before," I laughed.

There are funny memes that talk about pizza being a spirit animal, but in all seriousness, we can receive messages through our dreams and interactions with all kinds of animals. One night, I dreamed that I was sitting on a sectional in my living room watching a documentary about polar bears with U2's front man Bono. We were really into watching the bears when I looked at him in my dream and asked him why polar bears. Looking at me with a smile, he said it was all about awakenings. I joke that Bono is my spirit animal.

Maggie e-mailed me a few months later to tell me that her trip helping at the sloth sanctuary changed her life and her perception on what she was supposed to do career wise. Interestingly enough, she found out that the day of our appointment a sloth had passed away and wondered if I had truly connected to a sloth from the Other Side, and it wasn't just symbolic.

ROWA

Years ago, I was giving a lecture with many other spiritual advisors. One of those was a man named Rowa. Rowa was a veterinarian who helped underprivileged farmers and different Native American tribes with their livestock and pets. He, himself, was a man with deep-seated Native American blood. Although he wore a green Oxford and crisp dark jeans, it was his energy that exuded, if not shined out, his proud heritage. He spoke to the audience as if he was speaking to everyone individually. His background story was not an easy one. He was what he defined as biracial, with his mother being Irish. He smiled, pointed to his dimple and then to his electric blue eyes, and joked that they were hard to hide in the tribe. He was, however, accepted as full blood, as was his mother who was not of Native American blood at all.

"Why the acceptance?" he asked the audience. "Because our blood is the same. We've chosen to take human form on the physical plane. Our intent to living is simple; it is to love and to receive love. Our greatest teachers of that are animals. They are the cats that sit on our lap, the dogs that greet us at the door. They are the horses that nudge our hands, the birds that sing us their sweet songs. We make the wolf bigger than what he is. It is humans who make him hate, not the wolf itself."

This made me think of growing up in Detroit, Michigan, when it wasn't cool to say you were from Detroit. I didn't grow up in a pretty suburb of, but actually Detroit. Born three years after the 1967 Detroit Riots, I was often told that I missed seeing the greatness that Detroit was. It is said that Detroit is still trying to recover from the aftermath of 1967.

I have a mirror and I know what I look like. I'm as white as they come with the Irish/Scottish/German blood in me. I walk by a pizza oven and turn a shade of red. My neighbor across the street from where I grew up were what society at the time called a "colored." Although the *N* word was inappropriately thrown around often, "colored" or "brown" was somehow better. Keisha and I became fast friends despite our skin tones. She was fascinated by me wanting to lather baby oil on my skin and lay in the sun to become brown and I was fascinated by her mom cooking up grits for breakfast while her hair was being ironed, as in with a real iron that my mom used on shirts. She tried to tan with me and I begged her mom to iron my already straight blonde hair. Keisha would put her arm up against mine and tell me there was no difference—we both bled and we both loved. And we loved that our names both started with a *K*. We were sisters.

The two of us walked to the neighborhood block store one day to get a treat when a group of older kids began to throw rocks at Keisha.

"Why are you hanging out with a colored?" they yelled at me. "You need to hang with your own kind."

As I helped Keisha back home, I was confused. She was my own kind. But it was Keisha that was bleeding, not me. Yes, we both bled, but she was being forced to bleed more. She was forced to have to try more. She was forced to rise above more.

I couldn't comfort her, but her trusted companion, a rabbit named Luna, could. When we got home, she immediately took Luna out of his cage and set him on her lap, where they snuggled.

"Isn't it funny how animals don't seem to care? Animals don't care if you're black, white, orange, or green. They don't care what your bank account looks like or what your political views are. As long as they are being loved, they are happy." Keisha contemplated out loud, "It makes me wonder if there are a lot of people who feel unloved."

Keisha's words and Rowa's wolf analogy spoke to me on many levels. Is it fear and hate that makes the wolf bigger than he is? Can we make him back to the wolf just with love?

I had given my lecture and was preparing to leave when Rowa came up and introduced himself.

"You are a seer," he said. "Don't let the fear of it create a pack of wolves in your life when it is only one lone wolf who won't bite if you don't take the bait," Rowa offered with a small smile.

"Thank you. I'll try to send them love," I promised.

Rowa stared at me for a brief moment. I didn't feel uneasy; instead, I felt as if there were rays of sunshine warming my soul. "Your totem is the great owl, Kristy. Do you know what that means?" Rowa asked, not allowing me to respond before continuing. "You will do great work, but it isn't about your work being notorious. It is through your work that you will help others achieve their greatness. Keep listening to your inner voice. See the signs. Trust your instincts. Embrace the great owl."

Rowa grabbed me in a big hug and promised that our paths would cross again. "You may not be what you define as an animal communicator, instead you are a spirit communicator and there is no difference between the souls of human or animal. We love. We hate. We choose."

That same night, Rowa's life ended. On his way home, a deer ran in front of his car and he veered into a tree, killing his physical body in an instant. He did keep his promise, though, as just a year after his passing he came to me in a dream. His spirit is just as graceful as it was here on Earth. Standing at his one side was a large buck, a wolf stood on the other, and a large brown owl positioned itself on his shoulder.

"I'm the helper of the animals." He smiled. "My work there is my work here. The animals work there is their work here. They do not whine or weep about their work; they simply work. They do not whine or weep about their end of life; they live. I don't want anyone to weep for me or believe my work on Earth was for nothing. I'm not weeping. I'm not whining. I'm working, but most of all I'm loving. This deer," Rowa said, gesturing to his right side, "he is not afraid that this wolf will eat him, because we are all one."

Rowa nodded to me as if asking if I understood, but I wasn't sure if I did. It sounded too New Age for me to swallow, but I smiled in agreement nonetheless.

"I will help you when you need me. I will help anyone if they need me," he offered. "You may not be what you define as an animal communicator, instead you are a spirit communicator and there is no difference between the souls of human or animal. We love. We hate. We choose."

Rowa had repeated to me the exact thing he had said after our seminar the year before, the day he passed away. I didn't realize then how much of an impact he would have on me and how his lessons, which sounded a bit like Yoda from *Star Wars*, spoke more truths than I could've ever imagined.

2

SIGNS IT IS TIME TO LET GO

Our pets can give us signs from the Other Side to let us know they are around. It might not always be obvious or earth-shattering, and you can actually ask your pet for a specific sign. Then be patient.

INDY

Stephanie grew up in the city with its big lights and noisy streets. She was in college when her roommate invited her to come home one weekend. It was then she fell in love with the country.

"You've got horses?" she asked in awe to Lucy.

"Horses, miniature donkeys, chickens, and ducks, too," Lucy listed.

That weekend, Stephanie traded in her designer jeans and expensive leather boots for overalls and galoshes. She held chickens, rode the horses, and pet the donkeys. She laughed at the silly escapades of the ducks chasing the new litter of kittens around the barn, and she didn't even care that she got dirt under her nails. Not that Stephanie had a bad upbringing, it was just different, and she felt as if she breathed better here, laughed harder here, and even had a bigger appetite.

"It's the country air," Lucy's mom laughed when Stephanie apologized for grabbing seconds and then third helpings at dinner.

Stephanie made it her goal to own a small piece of country upon graduation, but even though you have a goal it doesn't mean that life hands it to you. Stephanie did spend as much time as she could away from her tenth-floor apartment and stuffy cubicle, taking drives in the country and stopping along the way to admire the peacefulness of what she felt was a slice of Heaven.

Fifteen years after college, she now had a supportive husband, three kids, and her dream in hand. She finally signed the closing paperwork to their new home that included a pole barn, several out buildings, and 30 acres of land. The deal also included three horses, chickens, and two miniature donkeys.

At first, she was horrified that the owners would just hand over the animals like that, but their circumstances were quite sad. The husband and primary breadwinner had been diagnosed with ALS. They had never had children, who they could pass the farm on to or could help them, so they thought it was best to just sell everything in a package deal instead. After several offers, it was Stephanie and her family who they knew would not just take good care of the house they loved but also the animals they truly loved.

"You can visit anytime," she graciously told the sellers, who thanked her as they exchanged phone numbers.

Moving is a stressful obstacle, but moving and also having to take care of livestock is unexplainably chaotic. Somehow Stephanie and her family worked as a team, along with friends, and got it done, making sure all the while that the animals were fed, bathed, brushed, and loved. As days turned to months and months to a year, the family bonded with the animals and the animals to them, too. Every morning before work, Stephanie would go into the barn to do her chores, all the while wanting to pinch herself with happiness. She loved each of the animals, but there was one mare she bonded with immediately. Her name was Indy.

Indy was twelve years old with chocolate eyes and silky brown coloring. She had some chronic issues but nothing that wasn't manageable, according to their veterinarian. She seemed happy and was playful no matter the time of day. Indy mothered the other animals, even the donkeys, who were often plain pests.

It was a warm September morning when Stephanie noticed Indy wasn't quite herself. When Stephanie went to offer an ear scratch, Indy turned her head away. She noticed she hadn't eaten, and when she got everyone up and outside, Indy kept to herself.

"I'm worried about Indy," Stephanie told her husband when she got into the house. "I think I'll call the vet to see if he'll check her out."

Stephanie's husband joked that Indy was probably just being a moody girl, but something told her there was more. The vet came only to find nothing wrong with her at all, but he said to keep an eye on her eating habits and to call him the next day with an update.

"She's probably just being moody," the veterinarian said, mimicking her husband.

But Stephanie still couldn't shake off her intuitive nudge, and she pulled out the phone number she'd stuffed in her home closing package and dialed the number. She hadn't heard from the past owners since the day they got the keys, which surprised her. She thought for sure after all the years they'd had with the animals they would've come to visit. Her husband reasoned that they might've thought it was too painful for everyone and sometimes a clean break is the best break. When nobody answered the phone, she decided to take a drive.

Not normally pushy, there was just something nagging at Stephanie, so she drove to the assisted living facility that the past home owners moved into. At the reception desk, she asked for them by name and the lady gave her a sideways glance.

"Mrs. Hart is in the dining room," she said and pointed to the left.

Stephanie thanked her and followed the signs, feeling a sudden deep sadness. Mrs. Hart sat expressionless at a table by herself, nothing in front of her, and staring at the television set that loudly showed a popular court show.

"Mrs. Hart?" Stephanie said, softly touching her shoulder, not wanting to startle her.

Mrs. Hart looked puzzled for a moment, and then she recognized her. "Have a seat, please. George," Mrs. Hart yelled at a man across the room, "turn that down for a second, okay?"

The man nodded and used the remote to turn it down one notch, making no difference in the volume, but it seemed to be good enough for Mrs. Hart.

"Mrs. Hart, where's your husband?" Stephanie asked, looking around the room just in case she missed him.

Mrs. Hart looked down at the table without a reaction before speaking. "He's in a coma. On life support. I have to make a decision today," she told Stephanie, trying to hold back her emotion.

Stephanie had a million questions, but she knew that it was none of her business.

"Can I ask you an odd question?"

Mrs. Hart grabbed Stephanie's hand. "How're my kids doing?"

It took Stephanie a second to realize she meant the animals. "That's why I'm here, Mrs. Hart. Indy is acting out of sorts, and although there's nothing wrong with her ..."

"Oh, Indy. Indy was Walter's favorite." Mrs. Hart smiled. "You aren't supposed to have favorites, I know, but the two of them had a connection. She was always full of life, but I could see that when Walter's illness worsened, Indy reacted. There was a spiritual connection."

Stephanie nodded, understanding now why Indy was acting the way she was.

"I think Mr. Hart's spirit might be with Indy, and she sees him."

"I don't know how I'll live without him," Mrs. Hart flatly stated, ignoring Stephanie's message.

"You're welcome over any time. The invitation is still open. I can even come and pick you up. Okay?" Stephanie said, standing up and hugging Mrs. Hart.

With only the response of a nod, Stephanie walked back to the entrance. The receptionist asked her if she found Mrs. Hart.

"I did. I feel so bad that Mr. Hart is on life support and she has to make that kind of decision. And today of all days I come."

The receptionist looked at her again peculiarly. "I'm not supposed to say this, but Mr. Hart passed last night. Mrs. Hart knows. I just think she's numb."

Before Stephanie could react, her phone rang. It was her husband telling her to get home right away. He'd gone to check on the horses and found that Indy had passed away.

There was no true reason, but Stephanie believed that Walter and Indy belonged together, although it didn't help her own mourning.

"I know she's in Heaven where the weather is always warm and there's green grass for her to munch on and run in. There are fresh water streams for her to drink and jump over, but I'm still sad," Stephanie told me during her session.

Stephanie came to visit with her grandma, who had recently passed, but instead it was Walter and Indy who'd shown up.

Walter felt terrible, and he swore he didn't steal Indy away from Stephanie or her family. Indy and Walter just had such a psychic connection that when Indy didn't feel him in the physical anymore, she willed herself away too.

"I believe he visited her from the Other Side before she passed, that's why she was acting oddly. She probably didn't know how to face you, the decision was hard for her, too."

"That's why she kept turning away from me," Stephanie contemplated. "I loved her too."

"She knows that."

It makes no difference if you loved for a day or years; love and grief don't have a timetable.

"You have to continue to love, though. And get back on the horse and ride."

Stephanie rolled her eyes at me.

"I can't help it, that's a direct message from Walter, and I'm just the messenger."

We both laughed.

"Don't be surprised if both Walter and Indy show themselves to the other animals," I cautioned.

"Oh, I already know that's happened. I find it reassuring."

"What's with the dove?" I inquired, as my guides kept showing me one dove sitting high on a wire. The image wasn't going away, so I prayed it made sense to her.

Stephanie grinned. "After the vet came and took Indy, I sat outside looking over at the sunset, beating myself up, and wondering if I'd made a horrible decision to move us here. Then I saw the dove. I'd never seen her before, and I know that doves tend to come in pairs, but this one didn't. She simply sat on the fence and looked at me. A strange feeling of comfort came over me, and I knew I would have to stop with the doubting. Every once in a while she comes back, most all of the time when I'm doing the self-doubt dance."

Stephanie kept her promise with Mrs. Hart, and once a month she'd pick her up and bring her to the farm. Mrs. Hart became a surrogate grandma to Stephanie's kids, and the animals were delighted in having her around. It also helped them all as they grieved together, each for different losses, but a loss nonetheless.

Bubba

I sat on the hard ground helping my friend Mandy weed her garden around her small brick patio. The sun was bright and we both wore large safari hats to protect our fair skin. Her cocker spaniel mix, Bubba, waddled over to us. He plopped down between us with a groan, closed his eyes, and began to snore within seconds.

"He's not been doing well the last few weeks," Mandy said, patting him gently on the head.

"How old is he now? Sixteen?" I asked, pulling a handful of weeds and putting them in a bucket.

"He just turned seventeen," she answered, sitting back and looking upward, trying to wish away the tears. "Tim thinks I should put him down, but I think he'll give me a sign if he wants to go, you know? He doesn't seem to be in any pain. But then I also wonder if Tim just wants him gone so that we can travel and do things."

I took my garden glove off and laid my hand on Bubba's back. His energy felt gone, as if he had already crossed over but was physically hanging on for someone—for Mandy. I've seen pets and people cling to the physical because they were worried about their loved ones grieving and missing them. So instead of letting go, they linger and they fight. Often the close family members can't see the forest through the trees, as the saying goes. Bubba may not have displayed any signs of pain, but there weren't any signs of life either.

Bubba lifted his head slightly and looked at me sorrowfully with his large brown eyes, as if asking me to tell her. Tell her that it was his time to go and release him, but it wasn't my place to tell my friend what to do. This was her child. This was her love. How do you tell someone to let go of that? I typically only give out advice, psychic or otherwise, if asked, and yet I felt I had to make an exception for Bubba's sake.

"Mandy, I don't feel him here," I quietly said. "And I feel that your dad is waiting to help him cross over."

Mandy wiped the tears that had been falling away. Dirt streaks covered her cheek. She laid her head down on Bubba's back and held him. "I haven't felt him either," she confessed in sobs.

"Why don't you ask Bubba, or your dad even, for a sign that it's his time to go?"

"Like ask for a butterfly to land on me?"

"Sure." I nodded. "Anything you want that will make it physically apparent to you."

Mandy sat straight up. "Okay. My dad and Bubba would go out rabbit hunting when he was a puppy. He used to say that Bubba was his partner in crime."

I made a face at her.

She laughed at me. "I want to see a rabbit if it's time for Bubba to go."

"Just remember that you have to give it some time. Heaven's time is different from our time," I reminded her. "As in there's no clock in Heaven."

"So it's like Southern time?" Mandy grinned.

I furled my right brow in question.

"In the South they're never in a hurry for anything. They drive slowly. They talk slow. Just everything is slow."

"Sure, Heaven must be on the same wavelength as the Southern United States," I laughed.

There was no waiting for a sign, though, because just then a small brown rabbit ran out of the bushes and sat down in the middle of the yard, where it began to munch on some dandelions. He looked over at us and then hopped back into the bushes. Bubba didn't even lift his head, but moved his eyes to look at Mandy.

"So, there's my sign," Mandy said flatly, beginning to cry again.

It's not easy to let go of something you love so much; in fact it's one of the hardest things.

Mandy called her veterinarian as I held her hand. Bubba's doctor made house calls, and so, without the stress of the car ride and the coldness of the clinic, Mandy and her husband were able to sit with Bubba in the green grass, under the blue sky, and say their final good-bye.

Mandy called me the following week to tell me that they buried Bubba's ashes underneath the large pine tree in their backyard. When Tim was mowing the lawn, he found a nest of three baby bunnies right atop the same space. Mandy got her Heaven hello.

If you are going through a trying time, feeling sad, depressed, or unsettled, know that you aren't alone. You are not broken. You are brave. You've been through darkness before and you've emerged. As Elisabeth Kübler-Ross, psychiatrist and pioneer in near-death studies, once said, "Learn to get in touch with the silence within yourself and know that everything in life has purpose, there are no mistakes, no coincidences, all events are blessings given to us to learn from."

GUINNESS

Signs from the Other Side help bring validation and comfort. My mom often sends me signs by laying dimes in the most peculiar places. When the health of my best furry friend, Guinness, began to decline, I asked her to show me that it was Guinness's time by showing me nickels instead. I needed to change it up so it was obvious. It too was almost immediate when I began to find nickels everywhere I went, but that isn't always the case.

Not long after the passing of our previous dog, Conan, we decided that it was just too hard and too sad to come home without the greeting of a dog. A friend had suggested we visit a local farm that bred Australian shepherd puppies. I had never had an Aussie before, but I researched them and the breed seemed to be a good choice for our family.

I chose the male puppy before his eyes were even opened from a large litter of puppies. His parents were workers, because Aussies are known herders and that is what they love to do. He had freckles and was tri-colored with a white lightning strike on his forehead that made the kids and I think of Harry Potter, so Potter should've been an obvious name, but Connor wanted to name him Steve. The name Steve didn't make the cut. He became Guinness, since he was the color of the beer—black and tan.

Guinness was my confidante and protector. He loved to get into the sweets, but he loved to be loved just as much.

During a really bad relationship breakup, I told my ex that all I wanted was Guinness. He could have every piece of furniture, but I wasn't parting with my best friend. He happily parted ways with him.

Guinness loved animals of every kind. He snuggled with our pet rabbit Ginger, and he loved the cats. He simply wouldn't hurt a fly. He never chewed up anything or made a mess, but he did like getting into the trash, especially if there was crumbs from a sweet treat, and he could take a squeaker out of a toy in record time. He hated the rain and if a dog could tiptoe, he did. His favorite time, even as a puppy, was dinner and bed.

It also helped that Guinness wasn't a fan of most men, that ex included, but Guinness adored my father. All you had to do was ask him "Who Papa's baby?" and he would run over to my dad, climb into his lap, and nuzzle him. After adjusting to the breakup, moving, and slowly beginning the dating process again, my rule was if Guinness didn't approve of the person, our relationship wouldn't work. Now, that same rule went for my kids too, but Guinness was just another child, only with a lot more fur.

Guinney Pig, which is what he was nicknamed, would sit at the front door, disallowing any date from coming into the house and simply growling at them. It was different when I first met my now-husband Chuck. I warned Chuck that Guinness's approval determined whether we dated or not, as usual. But when Chuck and Guinness met, Guinness simply laid down by his feet in pure contentment. It was love at first sight for Guinness, but it wasn't reciprocated for Chuck. One time early in our relationship, Chuck came home with a coffee cake from a local bakery to eat for breakfast the next morning. When we came home from running errands that night, we found Guinness delightfully enjoying the sweet treat. Chuck was not happy, but Guinness was.

Although Guinness drove Chuck crazy with his protective barking and his sweet tooth, they were more alike than maybe Chuck wanted to admit. Ironically, they even shared the same birth date. Chuck did love how Guinness was so protective of me, though. Guinness was also incredibly intuitive and could see my nightly visitors. If I had visits from the Other Side and he liked them, he would simply raise his head in acknowledgment and go back to sleep. If he didn't like the visitor, he would snarl until they left.

THE BELLS

One day, I had been having a particularly rough day. I was still working at my corporate job, and if anything could go wrong, it did that day. The kids were with their dad and Chuck was staying the night with his mom to help her out with chores, so I decided to throw the load of laundry I did that morning in the dryer and call it an early night. I thought I would read a bit before falling asleep, but the day must've taken its toll on me, and before I was done with the first page of my book of choice, I was fast asleep. Just a few hours later, I awoke to the sounds like church bells chiming and Guinness whining. He repeatedly nudged my hand and, in my fog, I kept pushing him away. Then I smelled the fire.

I ran down to the basement with Guinness in tow, to find that the dryer had caught on fire while I slept. I ran back upstairs, dialed 911, and called the gas company. Within five minutes, the firemen showed up, only Guinness refused to let them in the house. He lay against me, growling.

One of the firemen bent down next to him, looked him in the eye, and said, "I'm one of the good guys." Wouldn't you know that Guinness moved over and let them in the house without any further problems. No more than fifteen minutes later, the fireman came out and said that all was clear and they had opened the windows.

"You're lucky that you woke up," one of the firefighters said, informing me that not only was there a fire, but there were high levels of carbon monoxide. "What woke you up?"

I had smoke detectors and a carbon monoxide detector, and for some reason none of them went off. I told him that I heard bells chiming and then Guinness roused me. He nodded and said he'd heard something similar from others. I gave him a crooked look.

"Angels," he simply said, patted Guinness on the head, and left.

Guinness was gifted an extra-large bone as thanks, and to this day I won't ever start the dryer if I know I'm leaving the house or going to bed.

SAYING GOOD-BYE

When Guinness reached thirteen years old, his bedtime would get earlier and earlier. Pretty soon, he was snuggling into his bed on the floor next to my side of the bed at just four in the afternoon.

It had been a tough year. My daughter got married and moved to North Carolina from Michigan. Guinness mourned her move. His age showed around and in his eyes. His back legs would go limp, his breathing labored, and his hearing and sight faded. I prayed that I would just wake up to find him peacefully crossed over, but he was brave and he relentlessly fought. Several years before, the veterinarian diagnosed Guinness with liver cancer, but there had been no physical indication of a disease. When Micaela came home for her grandpa's funeral a month after her move, he shook with excitement and cried. He actually cried with happiness. The whimpering was heartbreaking.

Guinness wasn't just a dog to me; he was like another kid. He hated me traveling and he sensed when something was amiss. He was very psychic, along with seeing the spirits that visited me, could also sense an upcoming storm, terrorist attack, or when someone was sick. He would chew his feet and pace to alert me, needing to be snuggled and comforted.

The night before the appointment with the veterinarian, my son Connor, Guinness, and I Skyped with Micaela, who was back in North Carolina. We had gone to McDonald's and fed Guinness a meal of cheeseburgers and French fries. Guinness's hearing and sight was just about gone, but his taste buds seemed to savor his treat. Micaela said her tearful good-bye, and I snuggled up with him for that entire night, my mind analyzing and overanalyzing the next day.

The appointment was first thing in the morning, and I sat in the back seat with him in my lap as Chuck drove us to the vet's office. As we got out of the car, he began to jump around and pounce like a puppy would, and I thought maybe I messed up, maybe this was a huge mistake. The evaluation, however, showed that he was now in pain and had something neurologically wrong with him. I made the emotionally painful decision to allow him to peacefully pass as he lay in my lap.

After the last injection was given, Guinness took one final breath, smiled, and was gone. The doctor nodded to let me know that it was done, but I could already feel his energy had quickly departed to the Other Side. I held him a bit more, sobbing, and gave him one last hug. As we got into the car, Chuck burst into tears and held me for several minutes before we went home. Then I had to give the news to my dad, who informed us that a half hour before, all of the animals started to howl at absolutely nothing and so Guinness must've come to say his good-bye to his brothers and sisters.

It was just a couple months after we said our good-bye to Guinness when I went to bed and found Cooper, our Siberian husky and Guinness's best friend, laying in the spot where Guinness used to sleep. He was crying. We forget that animals mourn just the same. Cooper and Guinness used to compete with one another on everything, just like humans. They would bicker on everything from who would lead in their walks to who ate their food first. Guinness accepted Cooper immediately, and they were true brothers. They say elephants never forget, and I believe that neither do dogs.

Thirteen years of barking was a long time to now be met with silence. It took me awhile to get used to nobody barking at the mail carrier. Even a couple years after, I would still forget that he wasn't physically here and call Guinness to come to bed.

Our previous home had a tiny bedroom and he'd made his bed right next to my side. If I got up in the middle of the night, I would have to step over him. After his transition, it took me awhile to realize that he wasn't really there, and I kept stepping over where he always slept. I would reason that it was simply out of habit. When we moved to the new house in 2016, one of the first things I did was tell Guinness that he needed to follow. That September, we moved into a home in the country with acreage, surrounded by livestock including horses and donkeys. When we chose the house, one of the first things I thought was how much Guinness would've loved the home and yard. He came from a farm, knew how to herd, and was trained on a farm. The animals adapted quickly to their new home, finding their sleeping, eating, and playing spots, but neither of our other dogs, Lucy or Cooper, chose to sleep upstairs. It was a month after our move when I woke up in the middle of the night to a whine. Groggy and confused as to where I was, I said out loud, without thinking, "Guinney, it's okay, Mommy's here. You're just at the new house." I got up and saw the dark shadow of fur lying curled up on the carpet next to our bed. Deciding that I should use the bathroom, I got out of bed and stepped over him when I realized what I'd said and done. Just as I looked back down, I saw the shadow disappear. Guinness found the new house just fine.

Itsy Bitsy

When we think of animals on the Other Side, we don't particularly think of something slimy or icky.

It was one of my annual Halloween séances when a lady in her forties was called up to the table to experience the table tipping, which is when spirits can connect with the energy of the table and move it. Instead of moving the table, though, a young male came through in spirit and I had to break the circle because I kept feeling something crawling on my face.

"There's a young male here who passed unexpectedly," I told the lady sitting to my right. "And he's showing me spiders. Small black spiders." I cringed.

"That would be my son," she confirmed. "He said if he ever died he'd send me spiders because he knew that I didn't like them and he loved them."

The audience began to mumble.

"No, not bad," she explained. "He was a practical joker, and it's just his personality. But, yes, he passed and ever since, I find small black spiders everywhere. In my house, in my car, on me, and even in my dreams. I know they are from him."

I warned my family afterward to never do that to me, but for this lady it was an obvious sign that her son was around. Not every sign we receive is a pleasant one. Sometimes you get what is unexpected so that you do pay attention.

PENNY FOR YOUR THOUGHTS

"Are you a dog person or a cat person?" Shelby's e-mail read.

"I can't believe I'm replying to an online dating ad." She winced, but answered back anyhow. "Let's just say the dog loves me and the cat owns me."

Apparently, the stranger thought she was witty enough to warrant a date for Saturday afternoon. She was telling the truth, though. They say that some people are dog people, and others cat people. Shelby never knew why you couldn't just be animal people.

She had a dog named Mutt, although he was at her parent's house until she got a bigger place. It was her blond-colored cat named Penny that had her heart. Sure, cats usually didn't come when called, but Penny met her at the door just like a dog would. And when she wasn't feeling well, it was almost creepy how Penny would just know and cuddle up. The previous year, Shelby had had knee surgery and Penny instinctively would cuddle as close to her knee as she could without hurting her, and she swore it felt better.

"I wonder if he'll think I'm strange if I tell him I sing to you," Shelby laughed, rubbing Penny behind the ears, only to be met with a quick meow. "I agree. Maybe hold off telling him our love of Broadway until the second date."

There wasn't just a second date, though, there was a wedding date a year later.

Zac had a large Cape Cod that he inherited from his grandparents and so Shelby, Mutt, and Penny joined him and his dog, Alfred. The gang famously got along right from the beginning. Penny wasn't afraid of the dogs, and it was agreed that it was Penny that ruled the house. *Cats rule, dogs drool*, Shelby would joke that Penny was telling them this with her squinty eyes.

It was only a month after the move when Penny began howling in the middle of the night. Despite trying to calm her, she'd stare and scream. It became a nightly event, so Shelby took her to the doctor thinking maybe something was wrong, but Penny was given the all clear.

"Probably just the adjustment to the move," Penny's doctor said. "But, I have something kind of odd to ask. Were there any passings in the new house?"

Shelby eyes grew big. "You mean is the house haunted?"

"I guess you can say that's what I mean, kind of. You see, cats are known protectors. They sense energy and have a built-in intuition. There've been studies done to see if perhaps cats can sense electromagnetic fields or EMFs. It's like static electricity, and when it's heightened it might signify something supernatural. If you watch the paranormal shows, you might see someone holding an instrument that lights up to measure EMFs. Cats are sort of a natural EMF detector."

Shelby did believe in the paranormal, but she was astounded her veterinarian did too. She decided not to say anything, and instead met with me soon after.

"Shelby, there's a lady standing here who says you live in her house. She loves that you love her boy."

Shelby smiled. "Zac's grandma. Please tell her we love her house and hope she's happy with us being there!"

"She keeps showing me pennies. Does she send your husband pennies as a sign?"

Shelby sat for a moment and thought, but shook her head no. "He's never mentioned it. I'm not sure what that is. Maybe it will come later, though."

Grandma wasn't letting it go, though, and then she showed me a cat running around the house.

"Do you have a cat?" I questioned.

Shelby cackled. "Penny. Oh my gosh, she's the reason I'm here. Blonde moment!"

I joined in her giggles, but it wasn't just a blonde moment. I call it *psychic amnesia*. It is common for people to forget important names, birth dates, and meaningful information during a session. I attributed it to the vibrational altitude of spirit.

"So she wants to talk about Penny. I do believe they are seeing one another, which isn't a big deal, but she says it's a big deal."

That's when Shelby explained the noisy nights.

"There's something about an unfinished burial. Are they buried? Is there a tombstone?"

Shelby wasn't sure, but said she'd ask Zac when she got home.

"Also, I think Penny needs to go to the doctor. I'm not allowed to give medical advice, but I'm being shown a tumor in the tummy area, maybe urinary tract.

"I just took her, Kristy. She's fine. But maybe it will make sense later."

When Shelby got home from our appointment, she informed Zac that Penny was just a ghost hunter. She meant it to be funny, but Zac's expression hardened.

"What? I'm sorry, did I say something wrong?"

Zac grabbed Shelby's hand and took her up the stairs to the spot that Penny howled at every night. He opened a closet and pulled down a box from the top shelf. "Shelby, meet my grandparents. Nana and Papa, meet Shelby."

Penny dutifully appeared and began to howl, like she did every night.

"And this is Penny. Apparently, you've all met."

Zac gave the box of ashes to his parents on a trial basis to see if Penny calmed down, and sure enough, she did. It ended up that Penny was a ghost hunter after all.

A few weeks after our appointment, Penny unexpectedly passed away from a blockage in her urinary tract. That summer, Zac and Shelby took the ashes of his grandparents and Penny's ashes and spread them at the family cottage by the lake. As they walked off the beach, Zac told Shelby to look down. There on the sand was the shiniest penny she'd ever seen.

"Don't worry, Grandma's taking care of her," Zac said, giving Shelby a kiss on the forehead.

Shelby has a jar in her kitchen that she's labeled "Pennies from Heaven" and each time she finds a penny, she puts it in the jar. As it fills up, she donates the change to a pet charity in remembrance of her forever Penny.

When a person we love passes away, everyone sees grieving as something normal, but grieving for a pet isn't always as accepted.

People we thought we knew and trusted often consider grieving for a pet strange, even silly. "It's just an animal," they might say. Your companion is so much more than just an animal and only an animal owner and lover understands the depth of the grief.

⚬ 3 ⚬

FEELING YOUR PET VISIT

Many pet owners claim to feel their pet visit them soon after their passing. This especially occurs during times that were ritualistic for the animal and owner—feeding time, cuddling time, or bedtime.

ANIMALS AND SOULS

My parents weren't particularly thrilled with my ability to communicate with spirit, as it was looked at as dancing with the devil, so when they signed me up for parochial school, I'm sure they meant well. Thinking that I was bored and maybe needed to be kept busy, and yet secretly hoping that my gift of seeing the Other Side would just go away. It didn't. What it did do, however, was make me question the religious aspects I was learning at home, at school, and in church. What I was being told about the soul, spirit, and afterlife compared to what I was being told and shown from the spirits I was interacting with, had different connotations. Being young only confused me as to which were right and which were wrong. Or was there a right or a wrong at all?

One particular religious lesson I was taught in third grade completely devastated me. "… And therefore animals don't have souls, and they don't go to Heaven," my teacher flatly informed the class.

Our family had just recently lost our silver colored toy poodle, so to hear that Pepper wasn't on the Other Side with my loved ones wrecked me. I couldn't help but start to cry right there in class.

Although my dad tries to pretend he's tough, animals are his soft spot. I suppose it is a gift that animals have on us humans, taking away the guards we put up that often make us our own worst enemies.

The story of how we got Pepper was that my dad's best friend had an elderly dog that he had to take to the animal society and have euthanized, and my dad went with him for moral support. As they left the clinic, a lady was carrying in a puppy wrapped up in a blanket. My dad commented on the fur ball, and the lady explained that the poodle puppy had a lame leg and she was going to put him down. My dad offered to take him, and she willingly handed over the curly haired dog. My mom was obviously surprised, but Pepper grew to be a healthy dog despite the one lame leg. In fact, he could run faster than most with all four, and we often joked that he was simply faking the paralysis for sympathy. When he passed away, we knew it was his time even though none of us were ready.

The timing of the lesson was interesting and I was confused. Spirits were coming to me, some with their beloved pets by their side, so how was it that they weren't in Heaven? Why would they show me that if it wasn't the truth? Yet why would my teacher lie to me?

"Kristy, stop crying," my teacher huffed. "Enjoy your pets now. You won't need them in Heaven," he insisted.

Even though I was shy, I was curious. "Why would God take something that we loved away from us in the place that is supposed to be our paradise?" I questioned.

The response was met by a stern look, which meant to not question it again. The lesson didn't sit right with me, though, and when my mom picked me up from school I began to cry again.

"Are you hurt," my mom gently asked, softening.

"No," I answered, grabbing her hand and guiding her toward home.

My mom had sight problems and went completely blind when I was about twelve years of age. We walked a couple blocks before I could explain my reaction.

"Mom, today in my lessons we were told that our pets don't come to Heaven with us. My teacher said that they simply turn to ash and that is that."

My mom nodded. "Yes, that's right. Animals don't have souls, Kristy."

"How do we know that?"

"Well." My mom thought for a moment. "Only man is made in the image of God. Animals are not."

"But animals are living creatures. They have a personality and they have free will, for the most part, and because of that I think they do have a soul and a spirit. I just think they do," I said defiantly.

"Okay, Kristy," was my mom's response. It was actually a response both my mom and dad would say when they were exasperated with me and knew my stubborn ways wouldn't be bent. On this topic, though, I wasn't going to be influenced. I knew what I knew. I saw what I saw, and nobody could convince me when they weren't seeing what I was seeing.

HI HO SILVER

My older brother moved out of the house to take a job as a radio disc jockey about an hour from home, and it wasn't long after his move when he found a kitten outside his rental home. He would often come home on the weekends and in tow would be this tiny gray tabby. Cats were mean and mischievous, according to my mom and dad, and they certainly would never get along with our dog, they balked. It didn't take long before we all quickly fell in love with (Hi Ho) Silver, who loved to knead on blankets and jump in your lap to rub your face. They say that cats are a lot like potato chips and you can't have just one. That was the case in our house too, after my parents fell in love with Silver. When my brother left again, Silver stayed. One Christmas, my dad decided to surprise my mom with a rescue Himalayan that they named Saint Nicholas, or Nick for short. Then came Amanda, and then Purscilla, but it was Silver who had a big space in our hearts. He was also our only cat that had outdoor privileges, as he was more like a dog than a cat. You would call him in and he would be right there. His favorite place to sleep was on top of the air conditioner that was in my parent's living room. He was privy to the cool air, and he got a great view of the outdoors. As he got older, he'd forego going outside for his window seat.

I had grown up, moved out, and gotten married, but Silver remained with my parents. It was a warm summer afternoon when my mom called to tell me that Silver had passed away.

"I heard a thud and realized Silver fell off the air conditioner and he was gone," she cried.

Because of my mom's blindness, she was confined to the house for days on end. Her depression set in as soon as she realized she'd never see again. It was her pets that gave her unconditional love, and they were sometimes the only reason she got up out of bed in the morning. I tried to console her by telling her that Silver didn't suffer and he was doing what he loved to do, watching out the window in the seat none of the other cats were allowed to sit, but my mom was inconsolable. Silver wasn't just a cat to her; he was like her child. In fact, my parents often referred to him as my brother. I also had a sneaky suspicion he got more for Christmas than I did at least one year.

It was a week or so after Silver's passing when I received a phone call from my mom telling me that she thought she'd had a heavenly visit from him.

"I felt a cat jump into my lap and then rub my face but nobody was there, Kristy, and you know that Silver was the only one who rubbed our faces!"

"Wow, Mom, that sounds like Silver came to tell you that he was okay and not to worry," I carefully suggested.

I heard her take a deep breath in before she answered, "I think so too."

Nothing more was ever said of it and I never brought it back up to her. My gift was an off-limits topic. I knew my place and I kept that place as well as I could, but I secretly loved that my mom had a visit. It was the only one she ever talked of that involved a pet, but I think perhaps it made her ponder our conversation those many years before.

My mom passed away January 30, 2006, after fighting a month in the intensive care unit after a heart attack. It was a couple years after her passing when she came to me in a visit, surrounded by her animal companions. "They do go to Heaven." She smiled. "You were right!" she confirmed. Believe me when I say it wasn't very often Mom admitted she was wrong.

THOR

Thor was rescued off the streets of Detroit as a puppy with four other siblings. My client Donny had no interest in adopting a puppy, especially a pit bull, but after visiting the shelter he found himself unable to get the little brown puppy out of his mind. The next day, he was filling out the paperwork and buying puppy food.

"So, Donny, now you're a real thug," his best friend Josh joked. "You gonna get a mouth grill and a gun and join a gang?"

Donny growled at the stereotype, but he was surprised in the middle of the night when he woke up to Thor's mouth around his hand. Not biting at all, but gently tugging him out of bed.

Maybe he is dangerous, he thought. *What if he eats off my hand in the middle of the night?*

But that's not what Thor had in mind at all. He simply wanted Donny to let him outside to go potty. Where he learned the behavior was unknown to Donny, but no matter how much he tried to dissuade it, Thor continued, never once breaking skin.

Josh and Donny were watching a football game on a lazy Sunday afternoon when Josh fell asleep on the couch. He woke up to a wet mouth around his hand, pulling him right off the couch. His scream startled Thor and Donny both, until Donny realized what happened.

"That'll teach you to fall asleep on Thor's couch," Donny joked.

The veterinarian believed that Thor's mom had probably overbred and Thor had hip dysplasia that had left him in pain and crippled. Treatments weren't helping and Thor was rapidly deteriorating, so Donny decided it was best to let him cross over, even though he was only six years old.

Donny carefully lifted Thor into the front seat of his SUV. On the way to the veterinarian, he stopped at the local ice cream shop and ordered a vanilla cone. It was the first time in weeks that Thor looked excited, but he was apprehensive until Donny held the treat to his mouth.

"That's for you, Bud. That's for being the best dog," Donny cried into Thor's shoulder.

Donny wasn't one for good-byes. Actually, he wasn't one for hellos either. His friends and family joked that they didn't know why he had a telephone at all since it was rare for him to pick up their calls. When the vet asked if he'd like to stay, Donny shook his head no, patted Thor on the head a few times, and dashed out the door.

The house felt bare. The quietness deafening without Thor's noisy snoring. Donny wandered around and picked up Thor's toys—a red ball that Thor would constantly place in his lap to throw until he had to hide it, the stuffed elephant with most of the stuffing torn out but the squeaker still intact, and the dog bed that he used during his last year when he couldn't jump up on the couch anymore. As he picked dog fur off the carpet, he wondered if he should've stayed with Thor at the vet, instead of being a coward and running out. *Was Thor afraid,* he pondered? *Did he suffer?* Guilt ridden, Donny dialed the clinic, but they were already gone for the day according to their voice mail.

"It's just a dog," Josh said when he dropped by and saw Donny drinking a beer and numbly staring at the television. "Go get another one," he suggested.

Thor wasn't an *it*, he wasn't *just* anything, and there was no replacing something that he loved. He didn't know how to explain it, though. Instead, he pointed to the door and asked Josh to leave.

The next morning, Donny pulled into the pet clinic parking lot and walked in, his hands shoved into his jeans pockets as he stood at the desk. He noticed a small white candle lit and a sign that read:

If this candle is lit, someone is saying good-bye to their beloved pet. We ask that you speak softly and be respectful during this difficult time.

Donny wondered if they lit a candle for Thor.

"Donny!" the receptionist said, surprised. "What can we help you with?"

"Can I speak to the doctor for just a second? I'm sorry for not calling and making an appointment," he apologized.

"Of course. Take a seat and she'll be with you soon."

The doctor walked out about ten minutes later with a couple that was crying, holding a small empty cage. Donny pretended to be interested in reading his text messages on his phone, trying to avoid any eye contact. He felt a gentle touch on his shoulder. He stood up and followed the veterinarian to the same exam room where he'd left Thor yesterday.

"What can I help you with, Donny?" Dr. Cinco asked him, standing across from the exam table.

"Umm," Donny stumbled, looking down at his feet. "I wasn't sure if I paid you yesterday," he lied.

"Thor didn't suffer, Donny, if that's what you were wondering. And I kind of had a feeling you'd be back, so I hope you don't mind that I made an imprint of his paw print for you. You should get that next week."

"Is it ridiculous for me to be so sad?" he asked, sniffing back his tears.

"Everybody grieves differently, Donny. Loss is loss. You will feel fine one minute and then you might feel an overwhelming shadow of grief the next. There is no right or wrong with any of it. Look, you and Thor were a team, and you lost your teammate. One day you might want to add another pet, but it's up to you if or when. A pet is a family member. They just have more fur," Dr. Cinco said and then smiled. "Well, unless you've seen my dad's brother. Uncle Rick is pretty hairy."

Donny found his own smile within the grief. He thanked Dr. Cinco and left, feeling a bit better knowing that he left Thor in good hands and he did okay.

Josh invited him to go out the Friday after Thor's passing. Reluctantly he agreed but came close to canceling after getting the mail. In a box was the cast of Thor's paw print that Dr. Cinco promised, and he fell apart all over again. He decided, though, that he needed some laughs with friends.

After paying the parking lot attendant, he made his way to meet Josh and a group of friends at a comedy club in a bustling city lined with bars and restaurants. Donny pushed the crosswalk light, which lit up the street so traffic knew a pedestrian was crossing, but just as he took a step onto the road he felt a bite on his hand, pulling him back on the walk. Just then a car sped forward without stopping. If Donny hadn't been pulled back, he would've been hit.

There wasn't a mark on his hand, but he recognized that gentle bite, and he knew that Thor saved his life from the Other Side.

CHEWY

The cold day turned to an even colder twilight. Not much was on Marjorie's agenda except dishes and watching her favorite television shows, cuddled under a fuzzy blanket with her two dogs.

Working until retirement had been the plan when she first took the job at the small town's grocery store so many years back. She worked her way up to cashier and all the way to managing the shop. Marjorie took things in stride, for the most part, and it was her calm disposition that made her such a valued person in the community, especially at the store. It was almost contagious. The employees would often say that the angriest customer could come in, but a minute with Marjorie and they'd be her best friend.

When a large corporate company bought them out, she had to interview even after so much time in the job. It didn't seem fair, but she kept her position, although it didn't feel like family anymore. So that November she decided to join her husband Bill in retirement. There's a saying that God laughs when you make plans, something she shared with her kids numerous times—it could be Joyce not being chosen for the cheerleading squad or Bill Junior not getting into his chosen college, plans didn't always go the way you'd hope.

"Plan, but don't get too upset if there are detours," Marjorie would say.

That cold night, Marjorie's plans were given a detour. "I'm going to let Chewy out, he's whining," Bill told Marjorie as she started to load the dishwasher with the dinner plates. Their toy Yorkie danced around her legs, hoping for some pork chop scraps.

"*Shh*, don't tell dad," she said, handing Chewy a piece of fat before he followed Bill to the door.

Minutes later, screeching tires startled her followed by an excruciating whining that had Bill and Marjorie running out their front door. A white car spun its tires in the gravel road and took off, leaving the furry brown lump motionless on the road.

"I'm calling the police," Bill yelled, running back inside to grab his cell phone, while Marjorie ran to Chewy.

He was gone. She knew it. Just as she went to pick him up, she turned to her right and saw the headlights coming right at her. She stood up, trying to get out of the way, but there wasn't enough time and the pickup truck hit Marjorie. She flew up the hood of the truck, only to be violently dropped back onto the hard ground.

Bill stood on the porch with his phone in hand, stunned at the chain of events. He yelled into the phone for an ambulance right away. But nobody could help Chewy or Marjorie. The first responders said that her passing was instant, her neck broken.

The driver said it was dark, but it wasn't, and Bill knew that. Not only was it still dusk with a hazy sunset sky, a lamppost lit the space. The driver, a thirty-something male on his way home from work, was distracted by a phone call, and Bill knew that too. As for Chewy's accident, nobody came forward to take responsibility.

As with most all funerals, it was sad. Bill's adult children stood by his side as he placed Chewy's ashes into the casket next to his wife's body. No matter the amount of love he was receiving from everyone, Bill couldn't stop feeling guilty. He was the one who let Chewy outside. He was the one who didn't keep an eye on him. He was the one who ran inside to call 911. And then he was mad at the dog, which he knew was ridiculous. Chewy never ran out of the yard and the only thing they could come up with was he was chasing a bunny or was being chased by a coyote or deer. There was no other reason for him to run into the road. It was a series of bad choices that led him to be standing there next to his beautiful wife of forty-five years and saying his final good-bye when they should be home on the cold January day, napping on the couch with the football game droning on in the background. It wasn't fair. As they closed the casket and began to wheel Marjorie out into the hearse, he could almost hear her talk in his head.

"Remember, Bill, our plans aren't necessarily His plans."

He squinted his eyes and pushed the voice aside. He didn't care that it wasn't God's plan to have her here with him longer, he was angry.

During our sitting, Bill kept his composure as he sat across from me, stiff and formal, but his energy told another story, as did the spirits standing next to him.

"I don't really believe in this … ," Bill said, waving his hands in the air in a hocus pocus fashion.

"That's okay." I smiled. "You don't need to believe for it to exist. It makes it easier for me, and for them, but it isn't necessary."

If I had a dollar for everybody who said that to me in a day … well, it would be a lot.

His wife stood next to him in spirit, smirking. She was obviously irritated as she attempted communication with me. With his lack of openness and her frustration, I knew this session wasn't going to be an easy one. She showed me that she'd passed quickly, in an accident, and she kept showing me a really fuzzy small brown dog.

"Bill, she passed from a car accident?" It sounded like a question, but I knew that was what she was trying to tell me. Bill only stared at me, so I stated it again. "She said she passed away instantly after being hit by a car. She says she was gone."

Bill still just stared at me, so I continued and prayed that I was on the right path.

"There's a little dog that kind of looks like Toto with her and something about she needed to be saved and she couldn't do it. She's sorry. She also says that you see them both. That you really are seeing them both. Don't be mad, she says."

Bill's eyes grew wide as tears formed. He whispered, "She's really here?"

I nodded and pointed over to where she was standing in spirit.

"That would be Marjorie and Chewy, who's a he, not a she," Bill corrected me. "I'm not mad. I'm sad. I can't get through this, Kristy. I feel like it's my fault and there's a void. Such a deep void. I'm simply walking around in a state of numbness, waiting for my time. Is it my time soon? Please tell me that it's my time soon."

It wasn't Bill's time, nor would it be for a long time. Marjorie and Chewy weren't there to retrieve him, they were there to console him.

"Your pup says he jumped on your bed and you actually saw him."

Bill started to deny it when something in his energy wavered. "It was the night after they were hit by the car. I felt something jump on the bed, and there stood Chewy right on top of me. He looked me in the eyes and then disappeared. I wasn't asleep, so I know that I wasn't dreaming. I admit that I was spooked all night long."

"Your wife says that you have bells hanging from your back door and that they still ring," I shared.

Bill nodded. "We trained Chewy from a puppy to ring the bells to tell us he had to go out. The bell rings every once in a while. Instinctively I get up to let him out, but he's nowhere near the door. Then I remember." Bill's voice faded back into grief.

We are taught that death is final. It's the end. We grieve and we get over it eventually.

Bull.

Death is far from final. It's not the end, it's a new beginning— for everyone. And we don't ever get over it. We walk through it. And then we walk backward and through it again. And sometimes we stop in the middle until someone pulls us through. Hopefully there's someone there to pull us through. There's no time frame. Just as you have a unique fingerprint, your grief fingerprint is unique too. The corporate world gives us three days to "get over it" and mourn. Our hearts and souls tell us it will be a lifetime until we see our loved one again. The hurt is real. The heartache is crushing. And grief is one of the hardest things you will ever do.

Bill was still in the beginning stages of grief and, although I could bring through the connection, I couldn't take the pain away. What I did do was open up the line of communication with his wife and his pup, but he wanted more from me. It wasn't up to me to give him all the answers. I did help him recognize his signs, and after a year plus, Bill does now see the signs. They've helped break his frown so he sometimes smiles. He believes now—not in any hocus pocus, not in me, but that death isn't final. Death is like stepping into a different dimension, and there are visiting hours, it's just not how we think of it here.

Not everyone will be convinced there is another side. Some will be skeptical and cynical. And that is okay. Sometimes the grief is numbing and that is the way they deal. It isn't up to me or you to convince anyone otherwise. Sometimes they just need a kind word, a hug, or a positive thought or prayer.

We all will mourn and grieve at least once in our lifetime. We all do it differently. We all have taken moments for granted, thinking there would be a later, a tomorrow, a next week. If anything, death has taught us it's important to love and to speak the love because there are no guarantees.

Pastor Chris

My daughter married her high school sweetheart in 2014 and moved out of state to be with him, as he was in the military and stationed in North Carolina. For the past couple years, we've been blessed to have them home for the holidays, but for Christmas 2016 it just wasn't possible. It would be my first Christmas ever without my daughter. *She's alive and well,* I kept telling myself every time I got sad, *and so is her husband. I have absolutely no right to feel down.* But my heart wasn't listening.

Deciding to take my mind off of my depression, I ran to our local grocery store to pick up some items so I could start my baking. I moped around the store while my husband Chuck ran to get me a hot chocolate, because in his mind chocolate was going to make it better. It was an adorable and appreciated gesture. I stood in one checkout lane but I felt pulled to move to another, so I backed my cart up and pulled into a lane right behind an elderly man. We had gotten a big snowstorm the day before and his cart only had a few salt bags. I could see the excitement in his face when he turned around and saw me there. He was lonely and now had someone to talk with, even just for a few minutes. All I wanted to do was look through my phone and ignore everyone but it wasn't my way, so I smiled at him, which he took as an invitation to chitchat.

"How are you, young lady?" he asked me, smiling. He wore a heavy canvas coat and a winter hat, with strands of gray hair sticking out.

"I'm just fine, and you?" I answered with a lie.

"Well, my ninety-four-year-old body is feeling this weather, and I miss my wife and dog," he informed me, tears quickly forming.

My mom used to tell me to never ask anyone how they were unless you wanted an honest answer, and I found that honesty from this gentleman sweet.

"The holidays make it a hundred times harder, don't they?" I said, beating myself up all over again for my own stupid sadness.

It was his turn at the cashier and she asked if he found everything okay.

"Nope, I didn't. I'm looking for a twenty-three-year-old hot blonde," he joked.

The cashier, puzzled, asked him to repeat himself, which was met by laughter by both of us. "Sorry, sir, my dad is in the car and he's trying to find one of those before they get into the store!" I broke the bad news.

We laughed again.

"I wouldn't know what to do if I found one." He smiled.

"My dad says the same thing." I smiled. "It's the companionship, though. By the way, I'm Kristy."

His face lit up at the introduction. "My name is Chris. It's like we are twins, separated by many years."

I gently touched his shoulder with compassion.

"I do miss her, though. We were married for more than fifty years. I still wear my wedding ring," he said, holding up his ring finger. He waited at the end of the checkout while my items were being rung up.

"Can I show you her picture?" he asked, sheepishly.

"I would love to see her picture." I put my bags into the cart and we walked away from the cashier so we didn't hold up the line anymore than we were. There was no fancy phone, instead he pulled out his wallet and flipped to a picture of his wife, himself, and a fuzzy small dog.

"We didn't have any kids," he explained. "I was a minister and my congregation was my family. They were all my kids," he said thoughtfully. "I'm old now and everyone's moved on. I wish we'd had kids now. She wanted them too, you know? I was being sensible about money and time, and maybe a bit selfish now that I think about it. Do you have kids, Kristy?"

I told him that I did, and he asked me how old and asked me where they were.

"Connor and Molly are away at college, Cora is married and busy, and Micaela is married and living out of state," I told him.

"You aren't old enough to have grown-up kids," Chris gawked.

"Now, if only I were a hot blonde and not married," I joked with him. "But seriously, thank you."

I shared with him that I was sad too because they were older, with their own lives and busy.

"Do you think she's with me?" Chris asked, switching the conversation back to his wife and turning melancholy.

I hadn't told him my profession, and I was a bit hesitant anyhow, as he told me that he was a minister—some were accepting, others weren't. I could see the spirit of his wife standing next to him, with his mother next to her, and not just one dog but two.

"I know she is with you, Chris. I bet she misses you too and wears her wedding ring on the Other Side."

"Glinda was her name, like the good witch. She was a beauty. And faithful." His eyes glazed over with memories.

"Chris, you showed me the brown doggie in the picture, but did you have a white one, too?"

The elderly man looked at me with a wide grin. "We did long ago, right when we were married. I brought him home for her for Christmas. How did you know that?"

I just offered a wink in response.

"His name wasn't Gabriel was it?"

"Oh my, now you are freaking me out! Are you a psychic or something?"

I laughed in response and nodded, but I don't think he thought I was serious and I don't think he believed me.

"Glinda had quite the sixth sense, too. She would feel Gabby jump on the bed and tell me about it. I never had the experience. I would tease her about it." His voice grew soft again.

"But now you feel all of them around you, don't you, Chris?"

"I do. Sometimes I feel her get into bed and lie next to me. And I've felt a dog, I don't know which one, but it lies on my feet. I've never seen them, I just feel them. That probably sounds nuts, doesn't it?"

"Not at all." I smiled.

"I think death teaches us lessons, but I was never good at school so I'm not sure what I'm supposed to learn," he joked, although his eyes were hazy with memories.

Chuck was waving his arms toward me, holding up the hot chocolate.

"Can I give you a hug?" Chris shyly asked.

I wrapped my arms around him tight as we both teared up.

"You know," Chris put his winter cap back on, "you are allowed to be sad too. No one needs to measure their sadness against another," he told me.

I nodded my thanks. "You have a Merry Christmas. And never doubt that Glinda and the doggies are with you, because they are."

"Thanks for being a hug dealer," he joked with a wink. "We need more of those."

I laughed and offered a final wave as he walked toward the exit and I walked toward Chuck and the other exit.

It's easy to not move forward after a loss, human or pet, but in order to progress we must put one foot in front of the other and walk through the hurt, remember the happy, and find the present. Without forward movement in life, we get stuck in depression and sadness. The past is just that. It's okay to be angry and stomp up and down. Feeling is the beginning of healing. Letting go of the sorrow isn't about forgetting, it is allowing our loved ones to travel—to take their journey—and yet what we sometimes forget is that they come back to us.

Holidays, especially the winter ones, are tough for those who've lost a loved one. The commercials show joyful gatherings and celebrations, with family and friends around the table and pets happily lying next to the fireplace. The constant reminder that it is the "most wonderful time of the year," when in fact it is a constant reminder of loss, can open up the Pandora's box of mourning, depression, sadness, and guilt thought to be stored far away.

Many believe it's helpful to simply remind yourself how blessed you were with the time you were given. It's hard to explain that it isn't that you are ungrateful, it's that grieving sometimes doesn't help balance that into healing.

It's okay to miss. It's okay to be sad. It's also okay to find a new reality that includes being happy, creating new holiday memories, and new holiday traditions. If you can recognize that as you put up your Christmas tree or Hanukkah menorah, you may also release boxed up sadness, whether it's been one year or twenty years. Not everyone will understand why, but it's not their journey or their memories.

There is no time on the Other Side, so be gentle on yourself if your message from your pet doesn't happen immediately, and be gentle on them as they find the perfect means to make their connection.

4

UNCONDITIONAL LOVE FROM BEYOND

Just as you cannot destroy energy, you cannot destroy love. When our pets cross over, they wait for us to join them, but they also can connect with us in different ways before that time and sometimes to save us. The souls of our pets do not die and they stay as our companions even in spirit, loving us just like they did when they were in the physical.

FOREVER LOVE

It was impossible to resist the white fluffy face in the pet shop window and I immediately ran inside to visit with him. I wasn't a fan of pet shops, but after holding him in my arms I knew he was mine. There was no way I was leaving that mall without him.

I named the Great Pyrenees puppy Conan, after Arnold Schwarzenegger's movie character. He was going to be a big boy, and sure enough he quickly grew into a 150-pound lapdog.

The Great Pyrenees was bred to protect livestock, people, children, and any other real or imaginary predators that may intrude within the confines of their space. The breed is nonaggressive, filled with unconditional love, even tempered, and a great family dog. I had two small children at the time, and Conan met all the breed's finest qualities, including being gentle and patient. But he was a "fraidy" cat. He was afraid of everything from mice to squirrels to squeaky toys, but he was all filled with love.

When he was about five years old, Conan started acting strangely, so I took him to an emergency veterinarian who told me that Conan had heartworm. Although I had faithfully given him his medication, his primary doctor must not have calculated correctly due to his size, and he contracted the disease. There was just one treatment and that would require making sure he didn't move for days, it was very expensive, and there were no guarantees it would work. My kids were still quite young, and I was a single mom working two jobs. It was a decision I didn't want to make and then having to make it by myself was even tougher. The doctor promised that he wasn't in any pain, yet.

"Take him home," he told me. "Conan will let you know when it is time."

A few months later, Conan went into kidney failure. I held his fuzzy white head and sobbed as the doctor helped ease his pain until he made his transition.

"You do know he goes to Heaven, right, Kristy?" the veterinarian said as I placed Conan's favorite blanket atop him.

I swallowed hard and nodded, but at that moment I wasn't convinced. *Maybe I'm kidding myself,* I thought, trying to make it all seem like it was better than it really was to cope. I was second-guessing death and the afterlife and everything I was being told and shown from the spirit world. Maybe it was all an illusion and I was being punked.

I had to take an hour of personal time away from my corporate job in order to attend the appointment. I pulled into work just before lunchtime, wiping my tears away as I got out of the car. The maintenance man saw me and waited for me to exit my car and get my belongings. Bart was a war veteran with a tough demeanor and a take-no-prisoners attitude. Most of the employees avoided him and almost all were afraid of him, but he was always kind to me. I usually offered him a smile and small talk, but I wasn't in the mood, so I simply nodded my thanks as he held the door open for me. Bart immediately recognized the change in my demeanor and asked me what was wrong. Well, actually he sort of growled it.

I couldn't talk, though, and I waved him off at first, but I finally admitted that I'd had to put my dog to sleep. Bart's eyes glossed over with emotion and he took my hands and held them close to his chest in a tender way.

"The unconditional love our pets give us can't ever be replaced with any human being. Know that he will always be in your heart, and I bet he will visit you as well. He will give you a sign, Kristy, I just know he will. He will show you that he's okay and that what you did was okay by him. I just know it," Bart repeated.

I thanked Bart and we slowly walked to the elevator in quiet. The elevator doors opened, we both got in, and I pushed the button for the third floor.

"When I was in the military, I was assigned Jack," Bart confided. "He was a mutt of a dog. I never did figure out what breed he was, but he was loyal and smart. He was also good at sniffing out bombs." Bart's energy faded as you could see he was reliving painful memories.

"Honestly, I think I was given him because nobody else wanted to work with me," he laughed.

I smiled back at him, understanding that there was probably some truth to that with Bart's ornery reputation.

"He woke me up one day whining, and the doctor said he had cancer. I was hoping that he had something in his paw or something, you know? Something simple. They told me that he needed to be retired and he would probably be put down soon after. They took him away from me." Bart leaned up against the elevator wall and took a deep breath in, as if the memory still took his breath away. "I was called out for a mission not far from base. Kristy, my head wasn't on straight. Hell, I'm not sure it is now, but it really wasn't then. I leaned down on the ground and before I knew it Jack was there. I don't know where he came from, or how he got there, but he was there, and he jumped in front of me and landed right on a live grenade. I was burned, right here."

Bart pulled off his work gloves and showed me his left hand and arm. The elevator door opened to the third floor and we got out. I couldn't believe I'd never really noticed his scars before.

"He saved your life, Bart!" I exclaimed in awe.

"That's just it, Kristy." Bart stopped next to the elevator and didn't budge. He sucked in some air and continued, "I went back for his body or his tag or something…"

I wasn't sure he'd ever shared this with anyone before. I could see in his eyes that he was re-living every moment, a moment that I believe he'd worked hard to forget.

"There wasn't anything there. I got back to base and went to the veterinarian to give him a piece of my mind for letting him loose. The vet looked at me like I was on drugs. Jack had died early that morning."

"You mean to tell me Jack's *spirit* saved you, Bart? That's amazing!"

"I wasn't the only one who saw him either. Others did. This here." He pulled a dog tag out of his blue work shirt. "This is his tag. I still carry him with me all these years. He's the only one who hasn't abandoned me. Even after death." Bart wiped his eyes with the back of his hand and sniffled. "Ah, nuts. Well, that's probably what you think of me anyway. Nobody has to believe me, but I know what I saw."

"I believe you," I whispered.

"You do?"

"More than you'll ever understand, Bart."

Although not professional, I gave him a hug and a peck on the cheek that made him blush.

Nobody in my office knew I was working as a professional psychic medium and doing work with law enforcement on missing persons and murder cases on the weekends. Not Bart, not anybody, but I was receiving a sign of validation from an unlikely person.

As if wanting to protect me, Bart walked with me to my office. My boss was rarely a compassionate person. When we passed him in the hallway, he began to yell at me for being late, even though I had the time off approved beforehand. Bart held up his hand in a defensive movement, as if to tell my boss not to start anything.

"Her dog passed away," he said, continuing to guide me to my work area. I was afraid to look back at my boss, who was his superior too. Instead, I kept walking until I got to my desk and took a seat, but Bart didn't leave.

"Have you ever heard the story of the old man and his dog?" he asked, grabbing a spare chair and taking a seat.

I knew I was supposed to get to work but Bart's presence was making me feel better.

"An old man and his dog were walking along a country road, enjoying the scenery, when it suddenly occurred to the man that he had died. He remembered dying and he recognized his dog that had died several years before. He wasn't sure where the road they were walking would lead them, but he felt compelled to continue onward:

"After a while, they came to a high, white marble stone wall along one side of the road. At the top of a long hill was a tall, white arch that gleamed in the sunlight. The gate was magnificent, made of mother-of-pearl, and the street that led to the gate was pure gold. He smiled, they were surely at Heaven. The man and his dog walked toward the gate, but they were quickly stopped by a man sitting at a beautifully carved desk.

"'Is this Heaven?' the man asked, his dog sitting next to him.

"'Yes, it is, sir,' the man answered.

"'I knew it! May we come in? It's been quite a journey and we are both thirsty. Do you have water we might be able to drink?' the man asked.

"'You may come in, sir, but we don't accept pets.'

"The man thought for a brief moment, but he couldn't leave his dog. He thanked the gatekeeper, turned back toward the road, and continued in the opposite direction. After another long walk, he reached the top of another long hill with a dirt road with an old wooden gate. Sitting under a shaded tree was a man.

"'Excuse me, sir, we are both very thirsty, do you have any water?' the old man asked.

"'There's a well right over there,' the man said, pointing within the gate. 'Come on in and make yourself at home.'

"'And my friend is welcome?' The old man gestured to the dog.

"'Absolutely. There's a bowl by the well,' he said.

"They walked through the gate and there was an old-fashioned well and a bowl next to it on the ground. The man filled the bowl for his dog first and then took a long drink himself. When they were quenched, the old man and the dog walked back toward the man sitting under the tree.

"'What is this place?' the old man asked.

"'This is Heaven.'

"'It certainly doesn't look like Heaven. I was just at a place down the road and the man there said that was Heaven.'

"'Oh, you mean the place with the gold street and pearly gates? Nope. That's Hell.'

"The man thought for a moment, wondering if it was a test. 'Aren't you upset that they say they are Heaven?'

"'No, it actually saves us a lot of time. They screen out the people who are willing to leave their best friends behind.'"

Bart finished the story with a proud smile. "Gandhi said that *the greatness of a nation can be judged by the way its animals are treated.* I never trust anyone who says they dislike animals. Ever."

The remainder of the day I inundated myself with my work, sticking close to my desk. An hour before heading home, my boss walked by and simply said, "I get it. I've been there. Just go home, Kristy." My tears started all over again and didn't end for a few days. Maybe still haven't.

Telling the kids was difficult, but the hardest thing was coming home each day after work only to remember that Conan wouldn't be waiting with his wagging tail welcoming me home. Then the waterworks would begin all over again.

It was almost a year later when my son, Connor, called for me to come to his room.

"Mom, Mom, come here quickly. Come here, Mom! Conan is here!"

Connor was probably all of five years old, and I figured he was playing some game, but I went in and peeked in on him. Connor sat there, tears streaming down his face, while he petted the air. Or one would think. Connor was still in a toddler type of a bed and so if anyone with any weight sat on the bed, it sagged. Where Connor was petting, the bed sagged all the way down to the floor, yet not where Connor was sitting.

"Do you see him, Mom? Do you, Mom?"

I didn't, but I believed him.

"He has to go now," Connor said, giving Conan's spirit one more pat on the head. Then the bed bounced back into place and Connor and I simply stared in awe.

That was more than thirteen years ago, and we haven't been visited by Conan again. Although it technically wasn't my visit, it was Connor's visit, it helped me to believe that there is an afterlife for pets, and Conan was there.

Just a few months before Conan's visit with Connor, Bart had passed suddenly from a massive heart attack. I'd like to think he had a heavenly hand in helping with the visit.

Hurricane Charlie

"Reston, your prostate cancer has spread to your bladder," the doctor informed him. "You should probably call your kids. You'll need some support. Do you understand the severity of this, Reston?"

Reston nodded all the while lying. Sitting on the hard exam table he tried to listen to his family doctor that he'd had for years, but he was just hearing static, as if his doctor was talking to him from under water.

Numb and confused, he walked away with paperwork outlining a treatment plan and a list of appointments he had to attend, starting the very next day.

He didn't want to call his kids. He just didn't want to bother them. They had kids of their own. Jobs of their own. Worries of their own. He didn't want to add to their already full plates of stresses. After stopping at a restaurant for a hot roast beef sandwich and mashed potatoes, he made his way home, with cherry cobbler to go. Just as he walked in the door, his cell phone rang.

"Hi, Melody," he answered, wondering if the doctor called her even though it was against policy.

"Hey, Dad, I need a favor," she said from the other end. Before Reston could ask questions, she told him that she was on her way over and then hung up.

Reston put his cobbler in the refrigerator. He was never one for sharing anything. His ex-wife, the kids' mom, often told him he was selfish, blaming it on him being an only child. He thought she was probably right, but he would never tell her that.

Melody busted through the door about ten minutes later with a fuzzy black dog in her arms.

"What the ...?" Reston started to swear, but Melody simply handed over the animal to him.

"This is Charlie. We think he's part Chow and something else, maybe Pomeranian." Melody squinted, looking hard at the dog as if he was going to tell her.

"Oh, Melody, you don't need another animal," he scolded, pushing away the dog that was busy licking crumbs out of his beard.

"Exactly. That's why you need to take him."

Setting Charlie down on the kitchen tile, Reston furiously shook his head in opposition.

"Hey, what's this?" Melody asked, picking up the packet he received from the doctor.

"Well, Mel, this is one reason why I can't take your dog. You see …"

Melody wasn't listening, though, she was busy speedreading through the paperwork. "I can't believe you didn't call me. Did you call Scott or Jack?"

"I just found out today," he said, leaning down and petting Charlie's belly.

"Well, Charlie's housebroken and won't be any trouble. I can help out too," Melody said, grabbing her purse off the counter.

Reston smirked, clenching his jaw. Melody had a beautiful heart, but she always had too much on her plate and couldn't always be relied on, a promise or not.

"I *will* help out, Dad, with both you and Charlie," she said, wrinkling her nose at him, knowing he was doubting her. "I've got to go, though. Val needs to be picked up from volleyball and Brandon is at karate." Melody gave her dad a big hug and kiss and patted the dog on his head. "Oh yeah, I have dog food in my car and some toys and blankets, too."

"Wait, Melody. Where did Charlie come from?"

Melody held up her finger, motioning to wait a second. She ran to the car, coming back with an armload of supplies. Charlie ran over excited, his tail wagging while sniffing his food. She grabbed a cupful, put it into his blue bowl, and set it down.

"He was rescued from the flood waters of Hurricane Katrina. They said he was lying on the roof of the house for days until someone saw him."

"So he belongs to someone," Reston reasoned hopefully.

"Nobody claimed him, so either his owner died or is misplaced. Either way he needs a home, and for now he's all yours."

With a kiss on Reston's cheek, Melody ran out the door, calling for him to let her know the next day how everything went with Charlie and his doctor appointment.

It didn't take long for Charlie to make himself at home. Just as soon as Reston got his cherry cobbler out of the refrigerator and added some whipped cream, he walked in to see the dog laying on the couch, belly up and snoring.

"*Mi casa es su casa,* but move on over." Reston laughed and skootched the fuzzy animal over, reaching for the television remote to search for a comedy or game show, something to simply take his mind off the crazy day.

Charlie promptly snuggled up against Reston, laying his head in his lap. He looked up at him with sorrowful puppy dog eyes and licked his lips.

"Here." Reston scooped up some cherry cobbler with his fingers and let Charlie lick it. "You're good, Hurricane Charlie. You're good."

Reston didn't want to go to his morning appointment, but he knew the seriousness of it, especially when Janet, his ex-wife, called him right when he was getting into bed and scolded him for not talking to the kids. *Kids,* he laughed to himself. The youngest was thirty-three. He did, however, understand where Janet was coming from. Janet called that morning to remind him again.

"She never did trust me, Charlie boy. And no reason not to either," he sighed.

It was the truth too. She always thought he was cheating or hiding money. The reality was it was Janet who was cheating and hiding money, and yet when he found out he couldn't leave her. It wasn't his way. It was her way, though, and she dutifully packed his bags and put them out on the porch.

"After twenty-five years of marriage. I even bought her the fancy anniversary ring she wanted, thinking that would make her happy. Nope."

Janet told him that he emotionally left her and the kids years before and that made it okay. She just needed love. Maybe some truth to that too, but Reston didn't spend a lot of time pondering it, at least that's what he told everyone.

Charlie looked at him in understanding. *He probably does under-stand,* Reston thought. *He was abandoned too.*

"I'll be back soon," he called to the dog, who, instead of wait-ing, followed on his heels right outside. "No, Charlie, you have to stay. I'll be back." As Reston went to shut the door, Charlie darted out and sat next to Reston's feet. "Fine. You can come. Maybe they'll kick us both out."

Charlie happily jumped into the car with Reston. Riding shot-gun, Charlie pressed his nose up to the glass and took in the scenic view.

The hospital was only five miles away—too quick for Reston's liking. Charlie jumped out of the car and walked beside his new master until they stopped at the front desk.

"Sir, he can't come in with you," the lady at the desk snapped.

"He's a service dog," Reston lied.

The lady pursed her lips, knowing all too well the truth. Instead of calling him out, she pointed to the doorway.

"Well, where did he come from, Reston?" his doctor laughed when he saw the dog sitting next to his patient.

"You told me to bring someone with me," Reston said in a gruff voice.

The next hour was blood work, ultrasounds, and X-rays. There wasn't a lack of a dog sitter for Charlie during all of it, but the doctor did tell him Charlie would have to stay home the next week when he had surgery.

"I'll get you home as quick as I can, Reston," he assured him, patting him on the shoulder. "Just remember that you have to bring a human with you that morning."

Reston growled.

"Dad, you want me to take Charlie so you can rest?" Melody asked that same afternoon.

Reston didn't want Melody to take Charlie. For some reason, he'd grown close to the beast in just a day. Reston planned a busy week for the two of them. Between drives, the dog park, playing Frisbee, sitting on the beach, and eating out, they explored the town.

"I think he's done more with that dog than he ever did with you kids," Janet told Melody on the phone the night before Reston's surgery.

Janet was probably right, but what Reston wasn't telling anyone was that he had a feeling he wasn't going to make it through the surgery and that week wasn't just fun with Charlie, it was a bucket list for himself in a way too.

Reston did make it through the surgery. A week later, he was home resting on the couch, Charlie's head gently in his lap.

"All he did was cry for you, Dad," Melody said, fussing with an afghan. "I can't believe how much he's taken to you."

"You don't think I'm lovable?" Reston snapped. He was happy to be home, but he was in pain and didn't realize how rude he sounded until he said it.

Melody knew her dad's gruffness and shook it off, not taking it personal.

"Touché," Reston sighed, grabbing Melody's arm as she placed the blanket across his lap. "Thank you."

Melody didn't ask for what, but she knew that her father wasn't a *thank you* kind of guy and to just accept it. She smiled at him, turned away, and let the tears burn in her eyes. She was a lot like her father. *Make sure if you cry it's something worth crying over and don't ever cry about it again,* he would tell her growing up.

Despite aggressive treatments, the cancer didn't subside. Reston grew so weak that, after a lot of arguing, he and Charlie moved in with Melody and her family. Just a week later, hospice was called in and Reston passed away with his Charlie dutifully curled up next to him. As soon as Reston took his last breath, Charlie began to whine and cry. He knew.

It was Janet who came into my office just a month after Reston's passing. Although it wasn't Reston she came to connect with, it was her ex-husband who stood in spirit right next to her.

"He shows me a wedding ring on his finger, Janet, which means he loved you. He never stopped loving you, he says."

Janet paled and then her cheeks flushed. She bowed her head with an energy of shame. "I always blamed him for everything when it was really me. I guess we were just bad communicators."

Reston wholeheartedly agreed with all parts of the statement.

"He shows me a black colored dog with him, Janet."

"Oh, that'd be Charlie, probably. He's staying with Melody still. I know he's missed him. You know Melody took Reston's favorite chair and Charlie will sit and stare at the chair, his tail wagging. It's like Reston's sitting there ...," Janet rambled and then realized I wasn't really listening to her. "What's wrong, Kristy?"

I squinted and asked Reston to repeat himself before answering. "Janet, he says that he's holding Charlie. As in, Charlie is with him on the Other Side. The only way I see someone on the Other Side is if they've passed away."

"Can't be," she said flatly. "I spoke to Mel this morning and Charlie was fine."

I knew Reston could be difficult and not all spirits like to play by my rules of the reading, which included showing me those who've passed. *Maybe, just maybe, pets could come across as passed even though alive,* I thought silently.

"Well, please call Melody and have her keep an eye on Charlie," I asked.

Janet agreed that she would do just that and we continued with our session, bringing through more of her friends and relatives she wanted to connect with.

I wasn't surprised, though, when Janet called a few days later to tell me that Melody got up to find Charlie had passed away during the night. She found Charlie nestled in Reston's chair.

"See, I was right," Janet exhaled loudly. "He always had to have it his way."

It's easy to love and trust an animal, not so easy to love and trust humans. Pets give us unconditional love. They don't judge or criticize us. They don't care if we got the promotion or if we sing off-key in the shower. They simply love us and that love doesn't disappear when their physical body is gone.

The late Charles M. Schulz, creator of the Peanuts comics strip, once said that "happiness is a warm puppy." Reston and Hurricane Charlie are continuing their happiness on the Other Side.

Hurricane Katrina ravaged the Gulf Coast of the United States as a Category 3 hurricane in the early morning of August 29, 2005.

With sustained winds of 100–140 miles per hour, stretching across 400 miles of the coast, breaching levees and flooding 75 percent of the New Orleans metropolitan area. Thousands of people and animals in Louisiana, Mississippi, and Alabama were displaced from their homes. Although hundreds of volunteers worked tirelessly to rescue as many as they could, it's believed that close to 70,000 pets perished. On the upside, close to 20,000 animals were rescued, however only 15 to 20 percent were ever reunited with their owners. The animals that weren't claimed were transported to rescues all around the United States, in hopes that they could have a second chance for a forever family.

~ 5 ~

DREAM VISITS

Sleep is a wonderful way to connect with your pet on the Other Side. They can visit you in your dreams. Before you go to bed, ask your pet to come to you as you sleep. Don't get frustrated if it doesn't happen immediately. Make certain to leave a journal on your nightstand and when you wake up write down any messages you've received, even if it doesn't make sense at first or if the messages aren't coming directly from your pet. Simply jot down anything that pops into your mind, regardless of how much sense it makes.

JAY BIRD

Since he was a little boy, Pete wanted to be a police officer. Every single Halloween costume was the same, year after year, so it wasn't a surprise when he announced after high school that he was going to skip college and attend the police academy. Pete was someone who wanted to help everyone. His career choice wasn't ego driven, it was because he honestly felt as if he could make a difference by being in uniform.

He was one of the good ones, and some would even call him special. His warm brown eyes and easy smile made him a friend to everyone he met, and upon graduating at the top of his class, he accepted a position in one of the roughest neighborhoods around his hometown. With a lot of persuasion and grant writing, he convinced his superiors to allow him to start a K9 unit. Pete loved animals, especially dogs, and he argued that not only could these specially trained *dogs* help with pursuing fugitives, search for missing persons, and assist during narcotics or weapons detection but they could also help bring a sense of comradery among his peers. He was given two dogs—a German Shepherd named Marvel and a Rottweiler named Oscar.

Pete was excited and spoke of Marvel and Oscar as if they were his children, and in a way they were. They spent 24/7 together, with work, home, and constant training. Pete also volunteered his time at the inner-city schools, many of which had troubled kids; at homeless shelters; and at the local dog shelter, where he met his wife, Jodi, who shared his love of animals and helping. It wasn't unusual to see Pete handing out peanut butter and jelly sandwiches to the less fortunate on the street or with Jodi rescuing a dog from a burned-out house. He was a one of a kind person, never wanting praise or an award.

Unlike the stereotype of a police officer, he was sensitive. When Jodi announced her pregnancy by putting pink and blue ribbons around Marvel and Oscar, he broke down in tears of happiness. He went to the precinct that morning with a huge smile, announcing the news to everyone who would listen, still tearing up. You would hardly see Pete without a smile on his face, and his step was lighter than normal on that day. He couldn't wait to tell his regular party store owner, where he bought his lunch and pop every day. As he parked, he didn't notice anything unusual, but Marvel was persistently barking, which was odd for him.

"I'll bring you back a treat too," he promised and left Marvel and Oscar in the squad car, something that wasn't out of the ordinary.

Just as Pete got to the door, a man wearing a black sweatshirt and dark jeans ran out holding a gun. Both of them startled, the robber shot Pete point-blank in the head and then again in the chest. He then shot several times into the car at the dogs, who were wildly barking and trying to get out to help save their partner. Marvel was shot in the face. Pete somehow called in to his radio, "Shots fired, officers down." Pete and Marvel were both dead upon arrival of the emergency crews, as was the party store owner. Oscar survived with a graze wound to his ear.

The community mourned at the senselessness of the crime. Oscar was in shock, and Jodi was, as you might understand, devastated. Like most spouses of officers, she knew there was a possibility that this call would come, but never in a million years believed it would be a reality. She was looking at the future of being a grieving single mother and, for a quick second, contemplated ending her pregnancy.

The funeral was more than Pete would've ever wanted. Thousands of officers lined the streets and a special K9 procession marched through with Oscar leading the way. Oscar was handled by one of Pete's best friends and fellow officer, Dave. As the procession neared the casket of Pete, which also held the ashes of Marvel, Oscar lay down in front of it and began to whine, cry, and sigh in a knowing manner. His best friends were gone. Not knowing what to do, Dave let go of the leash and allowed Oscar to lay there throughout the service. Oscar laid his head down on the blue carpet of the church and cried through the entire ceremony. He remained distraught, so they decided not to take him to the cemetery for his final good-bye.

Jodi wanted to keep Oscar, and she asked Pete's chief to retire him. The request was unfortunately denied, but she was told that Dave was assigned Oscar. Although she understood the reasons behind it, she felt like just another piece of Pete was stolen from her.

The months of pregnancy were long despite the constant support of her family, Pete's family, and the police family. She decided she didn't want to know the gender of the baby. She wanted to be surprised. She was grateful when Dave and his wife Lori asked if they could be her labor coaches, and she readily agreed.

It was seven months after Pete's passing when Jodi's mom brought her to a session with me. Eileen had originally scheduled the reading for herself a year before, hoping to connect with her father, but the timing seemed too important and she gifted it to Jodi.

Jodi sat across from me, her mom next to her for support, when the spirit of a large German shepherd came running into the room. It sat there without a human energy next to him.

"There's a large police dog sitting next to you," I offered, not sure why I called him a police dog rather than a German shepherd. It was just something that came out.

"Is there anyone else?" Jodi's mom asked, hopeful.

I nodded as I tried to help usher in the male energy I felt, but it was dim and I didn't want to get frustrated and shut down the connection. I took a few deep breaths and asked my guides and angels to help him with his energy. Sort of like allowing him to plug in to them so he would have enough strength. Once I did that, his energy lit up the room, as his personality had when he was in the physical.

"He's confused," I told them. "He said it happened so fast, and he's afraid justice wasn't served."

Jodi sat there shaking, saying nothing, while her mom nodded her head in validation.

"He said he passed instantly and was surprised to find one of his dogs with him, and then realized he didn't know where the other was. He was in a place I often call the in between—not Earth and not Heaven."

"Purgatory?" Jodi whispered.

I shook my head no. "He said he was looking for you and for someone named Oscar and couldn't find either of you. And he says he'll be with the baby. Do you want to know what the sex is? He's very excited."

Jodi whimpered out a no, which I honored.

"He says to watch for the blue feathers or blue jays, Jodi. They will remind you that he and … Marvin. Who is Marvin?"

"Marvel is his dog that you are seeing," Jodi's mom explained.

I nodded. "Okay. He and Marvel will always be with you and the baby. And I know that this is soon, but he says it has something to do with who you end up marrying later, too."

Jodi laid her hands in her lap and let the tears fall.

"I'm so sorry for your loss." I offered my sympathy, knowing it wasn't enough. If I only had a magic wand.

On a wintery day the first week of December, Jodi gave birth to a beautiful baby boy that she named Peter. She could feel Pete with her throughout the labor, but she felt silly mentioning it to anyone. She was a sensible and strong woman, who was surrounded by many of the same types, but she couldn't help but cry when Dave handed her Peter after he was bathed and weighed. Dave bent over and affectionately kissed Jodi's forehead and whispered, "I've felt Pete here the whole time, Jodi. I know he's so proud of you."

A couple weeks later, Dave stopped over to check on Jodi and the baby. He had just gotten from work and had Oscar in tow. It was the first time she'd seen Oscar since the funeral, but she'd kept tabs on him through the chief and Dave. He'd had a hard time conforming to a new handler, they said. He wasn't just being difficult, he was mourning, and they wanted to give him some time.

K9's are trained and well behaved, but when Oscar saw Dave pull up to Pete's house, he jumped out of the car before Dave could grab his leash. He ran to the door, whining and barking in excitement. Jodi opened the front door and Oscar leaped up into Jodi's arms as if to give her a big hug.

"I'm glad I wasn't holding the baby," she laughed, kissing and stroking Oscar. He was a large dog, so she commanded him down and he immediately obeyed. As if he knew, he walked straight to the bassinet where baby Peter slept and sat in guard looking proud and protective.

"I think he senses Pete," Dave said softly. "Can I tell you a couple experiences I've had?" Dave shyly asked.

"Of course," Jodi said, and she handed him a cup of coffee and sat down across from him. She sat cross-legged and placed a blanket in her lap, smiling contently. Motherhood was more than she ever could have imagined. It was exhausting but fulfilling. She knew Pete would've been a fantastic dad as well, and after months of wallowing she was determined to give baby Peter the best life, with as many happy memories of his father as she could.

"It started a few days after Pete's passing. I started having dreams with him and Marvel in them. It was like he was lost and trying to figure out what happened. I could see him moving his mouth, but nothing was coming out. I started to think I was the crazy one and went to a counselor. She told me that I was probably having a hard time accepting his passing, but she said to talk to him if I had the dream again, and remind him of what happened and then tell him that he needed to go to the light. Which I guess is like Heaven."

Jodi sat very still, without expression. She'd had the very same dream and hadn't told anybody, except for me and her mom.

"So that night I met up with him again. I told him what happened, and told him I would care for Oscar, and that you, Oscar, and the baby needed him. I told him he needed to find the light and do whatever he was supposed to do in order to be able to move mountains over here. He still looked confused, and he still couldn't talk. I remember something my mom told me years ago when my grandma died. She told me to ask those in Heaven for a sign that they are around, and to be specific, so I told him to send me blue feathers. I'm not sure why, it was something that sort of popped up in my head. I'm freaking you out, aren't I? I'm so sorry!"

Jodi wiped away the tears just as the baby stirred, giving her a good excuse to get up and think about how she wanted to respond. Oscar wasn't so sure about the fuss the baby was making and looked concerned.

"It's okay, Oscar, he's just hungry," she reassured him as she fixed Peter a bottle.

"If you want me to go …"

"No, Dave. No. I … I don't think it's odd at all. In fact it's helped validate my own experiences." Jodi shared her visit with me and the messages shared. "I came home that very same day after the appointment and there was a package on the porch. Now, there have been a lot of gifts sent from strangers, and I've been so grateful, but look at this." Jodi held up a white blanket with blue feathers stitched all over it.

"What the …?"

"I think we are both getting the signs."

"Oscar is too," Dave shared. "But I don't think it is just Pete, I think it is from Marvel. I guess I am too. I sense him sitting in the back seat with Oscar. I swear I saw him the other day at my house, out of the corner of my eye. Oscar seems calmer when I sense him, so I think he sees them, too. Man, I'm glad you don't think I'm a fruitcake!"

Jodi laughed. "Well, I didn't say that!"

Peter was three years old when Jodi decided to go on her first date since Pete's passing.

"I just think you'll love him. His name is Jayson and he works at the hospital. And he's cute," Breanna told Jodi. "Meet us at Snarkey's Bar & Grill at 5 p.m. And wear your black pants; they make your butt look great."

Jodi rolled her eyes at Breanna, but she put on the black pants with a black sweater and looked in the mirror. Deciding that she looked like a restaurant hostess, or someone still in mourning, which she was and always would be but didn't have to look like it, she threw off the black sweater and traded it in for a light purple shirt. Pete always liked the shirt and said it made her blue eyes look lavender. Giving Peter a kiss on the forehead and giving last minute orders to her babysitter, aka her mom, she headed out.

As soon as she got into the car, she turned the station over from the typical toddler music only to hear her wedding song—Garth Brooks's "To Make You Feel My Love." Her heart stuck in her throat and she second-guessed everything. She was a dependable person, though, and thought it was unfair to bail on the night's plans. It didn't mean she had to commit to anything.

Jayson was nice, and the conversation flowed easily. He seemed sympathetic, but not frightened of her past situation or her present situation of being a single mom. They began to talk of their love of animals.

"This"—Jayson pulled out his phone to a photo—"is my dog Blue."

Jodi looked at the photo of a German shepherd that could've been Marvel. And then she put it together.

Blue. Jay.

A year later Jodi and Jayson married, with Blue and Oscar in attendance as their best dogs. Oscar was still having a hard time with Pete's death, so the department decided to retire him and offered him to Jodi, who willingly took him in. A year after, Jodi gave birth to a beautiful little girl. Although Pete and Marvel couldn't be replaced, she knew that Jayson and Blue were gifts from Heaven.

Love is a powerful energy that bonds people to animals and animals to people, whether they are in this dimension or another, and not even the Other Side can stop the connection. Pets are important members of our families, as they offer emotional support and companionship. It's natural and healthy to feel intense sorrow when they pass. It isn't just the humans who mourn, animals mourn for both their human and their animal companions, both here on Earth and on the Other Side.

~ 6 ~

SEEING IS BELIEVING

For some, seeing is believing, and although full-blown apparitions are rare in both human and pet visits, you might see a shadow, a wisp, or a silhouette of your loved one. The less you discount it as your imagination and simply trust, the more clairvoyant you'll become.

GREETINGS FROM THE OTHER SIDE

Earl wasn't the smartest dog according to Drew, but he was loving and friendly.

"I think he was Dalmatian and pug mix," she said.

I made a face, trying to picture what that looked like, and my expression made her laugh.

"Exactly. He was unusual looking for sure. He lived for almost twenty years before my parents finally had to put him to sleep. Earl was a happy barker, never meaning to scare anything away. So if someone came to the door, Earl would run and bark, probably excited that he'd get petted or get a treat, which our friends and relatives often did."

"Spoiled," I commented.

"So much. It was about a year after his passing, I think it was Easter, and Mom was cooking dinner for everyone when I heard my aunt come in and ask Earl how he was doing. Mom jokingly commented that she must be drinking already, but I walked in to greet Aunt Fran and there was Earl. He was sitting, his tail wagging, looking up at Aunt Fran. Aunt Fran was ghost white, cemented in her spot because at this time she's realized that she's seeing Earl, but Earl isn't really here."

"At least in the physical," I added.

Drew nodded in agreement. "Then he disappeared just like that. Afterward, Aunt Fran and I both needed a drink. He's shown himself physically a few more times too, but that's what I was wondering, Kristy, is he in Heaven or is he stuck?"

It's a question often asked, especially if you see the spirit. But Earl was absolutely on the Other Side.

Best Friends

Just as humans make lifelong friends, so do animals. Growing up, Brady's parents had a family friend who lived across the street with a pup named Tippy. In high school, Brady got a dog that he called Bowzer. Bowzer meant the world to him, and when Brady and Bev married, he became their kid. Tippy and Bowzer were best friends, so Tippy became what they jokingly called the step dog.

Eventually, Tippy got ill and was helped to the other side. Soon after losing her best friend, Bowzer's health also began to decline. Bev and Brady made the difficult decision to put Bowzer to sleep as well. After they got home from the vet, Bev called in to work, obviously distraught over the loss. Trying to distract herself, she watched videos on her computer, but out of the corner of her eye she kept seeing Bowzer walking around. Discounting it as grief, she didn't mention anything to Brady, even though she saw her several times throughout the evening.

"I saw her a few more times that evening," Bev said when she finally confessed to Brady. Instead of thinking she was being ridiculous, Brady revealed he had seen her too.

The next day, Bev was getting ready for work and clearly saw Bowzer trot by. "I said a little sternly, 'Bowzer! It's time to go play with Tippy!' and she looked at me. I was bawling by that point but I said again 'Bowzer! Go play with Tippy!' and she just disappeared. We've never seen her again."

PLAY BALL

When it comes to love, twelve years goes by much too fast. Cali was only eight weeks old when she was adopted by Carolyn. A beautiful Maine coon with tricolored fur and white paws, she was playful, affectionate, and extremely vocal. It was love at first sight, and she was quickly nicknamed Princess because she held court over all the other animals in the house, including a turtle named Chase. If you couldn't find Cali you just had to look atop his turtle tank. At almost twenty pounds, her family didn't know how she never fell in.

It didn't take much to make Cali happy; she just needed a dish full of food, water, a clean litter box, and her red ball. While most cats liked their catnip, shopping bags, crinkly toys, or bag ties, Cali loved her red ball. Grabbing it in her mouth, she would howl loudly until someone would take it from her, throw it, and wait for her to faithfully retrieve and return it. It didn't matter what you were doing, she didn't care, only that you played when she wanted to. You didn't turn down Princess when she wanted to play ball.

Of course, Cali was like most all cats. She loved her many naps, especially everywhere she wasn't supposed to be—the kitchen counter, the dining room table, and, her most favorite spot, the bathroom sink where she barely could fit. It didn't even matter if you had to turn on the faucet to wash your hands because she was completely fine with water. She had even been known to walk into the shower while it was on, and once she jumped into the bathtub while her mom was taking a bath. She didn't much mind it, but she didn't much love it either.

If you were watching television, you could often find Cali sleeping on the back of the couch, her tail wagging in your face. Like many cats, she enjoyed sunning herself on the cushion in the bay window, watching the birds and squirrels. Most times the red ball was with her wherever she lay, and when the mood fit her, she'd pick it up, start to howl, and find a lap to set it in.

When Cali turned eight years old, she began to lose weight and was diagnosed with cancer, but somehow she rebounded with treatments. The cancer came back four years later, this time her body was too weak to heal and Carolyn and her family said their final good-bye.

It was just a week later when Carolyn woke up to hearing Cali's howl. Thinking she was sleeping, she sat up and turned on the light only to see a wisp of Cali's bushy tail run out of othe bedroom. Remembering that Cali was gone, she reasoned that it was more than likely their other cat Bully, although Bully didn't have the fullness to his tail like Cali did. Just as she got up to check it out, she heard Bully running back and forth down the hallway. Sure enough, Bully was chasing absolutely nothing back and forth down the hallway. Or being chased. Bully noticed that Carolyn was standing there, and looked up in question, as if to ask her if she was seeing what he was. Then he looked toward the bedroom, but there was nothing there.

Crawling back into bed, Carolyn noticed something red on her pillow. Cali's red ball sat there, even though they had given it to the vet to have cremated with Cali's body. Yet there it was.

"We're okay, Cali," her mom reassured her spirit. "We'll play ball again when I get to Heaven. Until then, go find Grandma and Grandpa. They'll play with you, I'm sure."

Just then the room turned icy cold. Carolyn blinked hard and the red ball disappeared. Bully, who never slept with her, jumped into bed and snuggled up against her as if to give and receive comfort. Since that night, Cali's spirit has never visited again.

C-A-T

It was a beautiful Michigan summer afternoon when Judy decided to go outside and water her plants before they dried up. Judy was surprised as she started to water a plant she had sitting in her antique butter rocker that her father had given her. Curled next to the plant was a small kitten that didn't seem to care that there wasn't much room. While Judy tried to figure out what to do with the kitten, her phone rang.

"I have to tell you something funny," her sister from New York said, explaining that her granddaughters were bored and decided to play with a Ouija board. "Ask my dad what's on Judy's front porch," she instructed the kids, playfully. "The Ouija board spelled out C-A-T. Isn't that funny?"

Judy gasped and then told her that Dad was correct, on her porch was a cat. She knew that it was a gift from Heaven.

MITZI

The sun shone brightly as the kids wiggled in their seats, excited to begin summer break once the final school bell rang. A warm wind blew in right after lunch, bringing in a heavy mugginess.

"Alice, did you bring your inhaler?" Mrs. Birg asked, concerned.

"I left it at home, ma'am," she coughed.

Mrs. Birg looked at the clock. Less than an hour to go. "Do you want to go to the office?"

"No, ma'am. Could I maybe just leave now?"

It wasn't a frequent thing, maybe a few times a year, Alice would have some breathing issues and her parents just let her go home to rest, take her inhaler, or do a breathing treatment. She didn't live far away, Mrs. Birg reasoned. She picked up the classroom phone, and, with approval from the principal, she released Alice to walk home early, wishing her a happy summer.

It was just a few minutes later that the sky turned dark and opened up. Something about the feel of the air set Mrs. Birg in motion despite the lack of sirens. She hustled the kids out of the classroom, instructing them to take cover, yelling for the rest of the staff to do the same.

The sixty plus kids and staff sat huddled in the hallway as the winds easily peeled the roof off the building. After checking to see that her kids were physically okay, Mrs. Birg immediately began screaming for Alice, hoping she hadn't left yet, but there was no site of her. She ran outdoors to find the familiar unrecognizable. The funnel cloud had moved on and the sun had quickly come out, illuminating the destruction.

Maybe Alice found shelter along her route, she told herself. Without thinking, she began running along the path leading to the mobile park where most of her kids resided, including Alice. But the roadway was knee-deep with litter. She didn't even realize she'd cut her leg until she stopped to look around and saw blood dripping on her shoe.

First responders were there immediately. She grabbed the hand of the first police officer she saw, leading him away from the school and toward the park.

"I'm not sure we can get down that way," he told her. "It's bad."

Never one to take no for an answer, she recognized him as one of her past students.

"Lee, we have to."

He saw the fever in her eyes. Calling into his radio, he told his superior that he was heading to the park. They made the journey down the road, walking around rooftops that had blown off, avoiding overturned cars, and climbing over bushes and trees that were uprooted.

The smoke from some small fires was making Lee wary. There were downed wires and he was afraid there might be some gas lines that could spark at any time.

"God, please, if you are listening, I need to find Alice," Mrs. Birg cried out loud.

Lee was about to turn around when they caught sight of a dog running toward them.

"I think this is Mitzi, Alice's dog," Mrs. Birg screeched. Leaning down, she looked at the tags and sure enough it was Mitzi. Mitzi raced around Mrs. Birg and into a small shed that once sat next to a mobile home. Barking and jumping at the outbuilding, the police officer and Mrs. Birg pulled away metal and glass until they could open the door. There was Alice, covered by an old mattress, alive but unconscious.

First responders worked on Alice as the ambulance slowly made their way to pick her up and finally take her to the hospital. In all the commotion, Mrs. Birg lost sight of Mitzi.

Three people lost their life that day in the small Bible Belt town of Oklahoma, but nobody connected to the school. The storm came and left just as quickly, except the pain of the losses would be felt forever. It could've been worse, everyone said. The school was in tragic shape, and everyone who saw it was in awe that nobody was injured or died.

Mrs. Birg couldn't shake her guilt about Alice, though. Her co-workers consoled her, reminding her that Alice was fine. It was true, Alice was fine. She decided she had to visit Alice and her parents and apologize.

The Red Cross put up the misplaced in a hotel in the closest town, about twenty miles from the school. It was a week from the day the tornado hit when she made the drive. Getting out of the car, she immediately saw Alice playing with other school kids in the outside hotel pool. The parents watched from their lounge chairs, many with their laptops by their sides. Alice and two other schoolmates saw Mrs. Birg and came running over with a hug for her.

"Is one of your parents here, Alice?" she asked.

Alice nodded and took Mrs. Birg's hand, leading her to a shaded area where her mom and dad sat. They both stood up once they saw Mrs. Birg, and Alice's mom embraced her.

"You saved our girl. Thank you."

"That's what I want to talk to you about." Fidgeting with the straps on her purse, she took a deep breath. She taught to always take responsibility and she wanted to be an example to the kids. "I'm so sorry. I should've never let Alice leave. Even without the twister, she could've had a full-blown asthma attack, and I take full responsibility. I will resign if that's what you want."

There. She'd said it. She'd been practicing several times for the whole week and now she'd said it.

"No, Mrs. Birg. No. You saved her life. She's fine. All is fine. You are an amazing teacher, and we don't think you made a mistake at all. We just are very thankful for you finding her," Mr. Little said, touching Mrs. Birg's shoulder. "How did you find her? I mean, the town looks like a war zone. What made you open that door?"

"Your dog's the hero," Mrs. Birg announced. "Mitzi somehow found me and led me to her. She's a real-life Lassie! I just feel horrible that I couldn't catch her when she ran toward the woods. Did anyone turn her in?"

"I told you I saw her," Alice whispered to her mom, who had paled.

"It couldn't be our dog, Mrs. Birg."

"Well, it was. I even saw her dog tag with her name and address on it."

"Our dog died last year," Mrs. Little shared. "Alice said that it was Mitzi who led her to hide in the shed, and we thought it was lack of oxygen or the bump on her head that made her imagine it."

"Lee, the police officer who was with me, saw her too. You can ask him. It was Mitzi."

I was doing a psychic segment on a popular radio station in Oklahoma when Mrs. Birg called in asking if I believed pets could visit from the Other Side. Without any specific question, I immediately saw a Border collie type dog in spirit with a name that started with an M. I asked her if the animal belonged to her. Her voice caught slightly, and she said she thought she knew what I was talking about. She didn't *think*, she *knew*, and afterward she phoned to tell me.

"If it wasn't for Mitzi's spirit, that little girl would've died."

Mitzi wasn't about to let that happen. A protector in the physical, and a protector in spirit, Mitzi was still watching out for her family.

Alice indeed saw Mitzi. She followed her to the shed, making certain she was under cover before seeking out help. Alice's family calls it a miracle.

Rescues from the Other Side

Alice isn't the only one who has been saved by a pet who has passed. There've been many who've claimed their animal from the Other Side saved them from everything from fires by waking them up to going to getting help after a car accident. As humans, we tend to be shallow with an out of sight, out of mind type of mind-set. Our pets believe that love is eternal.

Near-Death Experiences

Many children report seeing their pets on the Other Side after having a near-death experience. Some believe it's the innocence of a child. Others believe that children are closer to Heaven than adults and their sixth sense isn't clouded by cynicism.

Near-death experiences are often thought taboo. Science tries to explain them away by factoring in brain trauma, oxygen deficiency, and drugs and anesthetics. Others believe it is simply wish fulfillment. It would make sense as to why adults don't shout from the rooftops their near-death experience, just as many intuitives keep their sixth sense gifts quiet.

Trevor was diagnosed with juvenile diabetes when he was twelve years old. He was a strong-willed, positive kid who didn't let the disability of diabetes prevent him from anything, including sports, which he excelled in. Once in college, he had some hard talks with the coaches and decided that professional football just wasn't going to happen. Not because of his skills, but because of his health. He was a risk, and he knew that, but it didn't stop him from playing for fun.

It was an autumn day and his buddies threw around the football before deciding to get some food at their favorite greasy spoon. After that, everyone was going to the movies, but Trevor wasn't feeling so great so he headed back to his apartment on campus and lay down. When Trevor didn't show up for class the next day, his best friend became concerned.

"He always answered his phone," Chad told me. "It's connected to his hand like an extra finger."

I smiled. I had kids and I knew that was the truth with almost all the youth and adults today.

"Something just didn't feel right," Chad said. "You know, like that gut feeling that told me I had to check on him."

I nodded, wanting to laugh, because of course I knew all about the gut feelings.

"He even called the cops, that's how strong his intuition was," Trevor added, sitting next to his best friends. "It's a good thing I was mostly dead or I would've killed you." They laughed.

Trevor had apparently gotten food poisoning and with the juvenile diabetes working against him, his organs started to shut down. When they found him, he was unconscious.

"They put me in ICU. Well, that's what they tell me. But I wasn't in ICU, or at least my spirit wasn't. I was in Heaven," Trevor explained thoughtfully.

"The first to greet me was my favorite dog growing up, Dweezil. And behind him were more—the chickens and hens that were on my grandparents' farm and Skittles, our pet rabbit, hopped up. There was a cat there too, gray and black striped. They were so happy to see me. The grass was green; the skies were blue. The weather perfect. It was like your perfect vacation."

"Unless you don't like animals," Chad joked. "That'd be Hell, right?"

Trevor ignored him, continuing to share his experience as if reliving it right there. "There was something odd, though. It was like I was visiting, not staying. Just a feeling, I guess. And then I saw my family on the Other Side. They didn't talk out loud, more like in my head, and they told me to just rest for a while. So I sat down in the grass and hugged my dog and rabbit. I could feel the cat rub up against my leg, and I had the most peaceful sleep." His voice faded into the memory. "Then I woke up to tubes, my mom crying, and doctors and nurses all around. And now here I am."

"I'm glad you are," I told him. "The cat, that was your mom's cat growing up, right?"

Trevor looked at me with his eyes wide. "Yes! My grandpa hated cats. They owned a farm and cats were good for hunting mice, not being house pets. Mom said she snuck the kitten into the house and it took Grandpa forever to notice it. The kitten took to ..."

"Grandpa," I finished, laughing. It seemed to be that cats love to antagonize those who hate them or those who are allergic to them and make them their favorite.

Trevor laughed. "Yep. Then one day this cat accidently got out and a delivery truck backed up over him. I never knew this story until I told my mom what I saw and she told me."

"What was the cat's name?" Chris asked, curiously.

Trevor laughed before answering. "Well, Grandpa was determined to not get close to the cat, so he wouldn't let Mom or Grandma name it. They called it Cat."

"Did your mom and dad believe you?"

He nodded. "They did. So did the doctors and nurses. They said I really shouldn't be here, but here I am."

Trevor's experience changed his life, like many who've had a near-death experience share. He switched his major from communication and decided to go into medicine.

I KID YOU NOT

"I really want you to meet Kade," Anita told Maddie, grabbing her by the elbow and leading her toward a bocce ball game.

Anita had invited Maddie to her house for a barbeque with what seemed the rest of her one hundred closest friends. Maddie had met Anita at a work function and they immediately clicked. But it seemed so many others clicked with her friend too, she laughed to herself, looking at all the people. Anita was beautiful, intelligent, witty, and she lived on the lake with her equally handsome, intelligent, and witty husband, Lyle.

Anita noticed Maddie was feeling uncomfortable. Crowds weren't Maddie's deal, which is exactly why she hadn't shared the fact that she invited so many of her friends and neighbors to an informal Saturday afternoon get-together.

When Lyle and Anita purchased the house, they knew they wanted to share in the fun of their lake life and saved for two pontoons, a speedboat, several kayaks, and other lake toys like the water trampoline. It was a weekly occurrence to have a group sitting on their deck, enjoying the water and the rays, and Lyle had no problem playing Captain of the Lake.

"No," Maggie groaned. "This feels like a setup."

Anita pretended to ignore Maddie and stopped in the middle of the green in front of five very handsome men. If Maddie could've ran, she would've, but instead she turned beet red and stuffed her hands in the pockets of her white denim shorts, or else she was going to strangle her maybe now ex friend.

"Hi, boys," Anita smiled easily. "Sorry about the interruption, but this is one of my best friends and I wanted to introduce her. This is Maddie," Anita said. As if in game show fashion like Vanna White revealing a letter, Anita showed her off and then touched Maddie's shoulder with encouragement.

A chorus of greetings came from the men, but all Maddie could focus on was ways to make her escape.

"Kade, can you partner with Mads? Bocce is her favorite game." Anita lightly pushed her toward a man she was assuming was Kade, turned around, and hightailed it back to the deck.

"I'm not a psychic, but I'm betting that bocce isn't really your favorite game." Kade laughed, handing Maddie a small red ball.

"You would be right, Zoltar." Maddie grinned.

"*Big*! My favorite movie." Kade grinned. "Hey, I apologize for my sister-in-law. She can be a bit ..."

"Good-hearted," Maddie smiled.

"*Pushy* was the word I was going for." Kade laughed before throwing his ball down the lane. "You want to get some lemonade or something?"

"Sure," she answered, handing the ball to one of the other guys and walking down the lawn toward the house with Kade by her side.

Although it wasn't a long walk back to the house, there was something that just felt comfortable, and he must've felt it too because when he grabbed her hand in his she didn't pull back.

"I'll get us some drinks and you find us some seats," Kade offered.

"Deal."

As Kade walked into the house, Maddie felt someone watching her as she scoured the crowd for two empty seats together and caught Anita's eye. Anita raised her right eyebrow and gave her a look as if to say *told you so*. She then pointed to a shady corner of the deck where two bright orange Adirondack chairs sat unoccupied. Maddie blushed and waved her friend off as she grabbed the seats. She caught sight of Kade looking for her and just as soon as she went to stand up to get his attention, a man with short, blond, spikey hair stopped him. Although they were several feet from one another, and she tried hard not to eavesdrop, it was hard to not hear what was said.

"How are the kids?" the stranger asked Kade.

"Good. They are sure keeping me busy."

"Man, I only have one. I don't know how you are doing it. Mine is eating me out of house and home!"

Kade laughed in response. "And I have a newborn coming soon too, so life is about to get a bit crazier."

Before Maddie could hear anymore, she got up, grabbed her purse, and started for the side fence. *Kids and a newborn? Do they think I'm nuts?* she sniffled. *I can't be hurt again.*

It had been just a few years since Maddie broke off an engagement with a man she was sure she'd spend her life with, have babies with, and grow old with. But a phone call alerting her just a few months before the wedding that her fiancé had been having a long affair and that his mistress was pregnant with her soon-to-be husband's daughter changed all that. She broke off the wedding and the relationship and had been in hibernation since. The overheard conversation was like a flashback that made her realize she wasn't healed and maybe she would never be.

"Maddie. Maddie!" She heard her name being called, the voice getting closer and closer.

Kade caught up to Maddie as soon as she reached her car. "Maddie, what's wrong?"

Maddie gave him credit for being assertive, but she didn't want any more drama in her life.

"Is everything okay?" Kade asked, exasperated.

Maddie shook her head as she opened her car door, but something within her decided she had nothing to lose and needed to speak her mind. "Yes, something is wrong. You are flirting with me and you have a newborn on the way? Really? I must have *I'm a sucker* written on my face."

Kade stared at Maddie and then burst into laughter.

Maddie looked at him aghast and mentally promised to never date again. Ever. Although they weren't on a date, this was a wake-up call for her.

Kade grabbed his phone out of his back pocket, put his passcode in, clicked around a bit, and then handed her the phone.

"Whaaa? What is this?"

"I want to show you my baby mama." Kade smirked.

Maddie was now angry, but she couldn't help her curiosity. She looked down at the picture and was aghast. "Well, that's the ugliest mama I've ever seen," she responded, looking at the picture. "And don't I feel like a donkey?" Maddie's face turned red with embarrassment and she laughed. Although it might be a mama, it wasn't a human, it was a goat.

"I raise goats," Kade simply explained. "This is Buffy."

"And that's why they are eating you out of house and home," Maddie moaned in understanding, holding her head in her hands and feeling thoroughly revolted at her eavesdropping and assumption. "I have no idea how to apologize, but I've made a fool of myself and I think I better leave." Maddie attempted to slide into her car seat, but Kade gently pulled her back.

"Oh no, you owe me one now. I ran and everything. Plus, our lemonade is getting warm."

Kade grabbed Maddie's hand and walked her to the orange lawn chairs. "I think we need something stronger than this, though," he joked. "Let's toast to new beginnings."

Maddie nodded and toasted her blue Solo cup with Kade's. "And to kids." They both laughed, but they were interrupted by a jingle from Kade's cell phone.

Kade looked at the number, muttered an apology to Maddie, and answered with, "What's wrong?" Kade's face turned white as he listened to the person on the other end. "I'll be there as soon as I can." Kade hung up the phone and stood up. "I'm so very sorry, Maddie. This is the worst introduction ever. That was my farm manager. Buffy, my goat, is in labor, but it seems like something is going wrong. I have to go."

Maddie stood up. "Let's go."

He looked at her with surprise.

"I'm not a veterinarian, but I'm a nurse and maybe I can help."

Kade nodded his thanks. Less than twenty minutes later, they sat on the barn floor with Buffy, who had passed away while feeding her two healthy kids, according to Rod, the farm manager. Kade sobbed as he held the goat. It was surprising to Maddie, as she assumed farmers weren't attached to their livestock, but this was obviously not the case here.

"I'm sorry, Kade," Maddie said, putting her hand on his shoulder in comfort.

Kade wiped his tears with the back of his hand. "It must've been bloat. I need to bury her and then bottle feed the kids before I lose them too. Hopefully I can find a foster mom. Rod must be exhausted."

Carefully, Kade picked up Buffy while Maddie followed. Rod had already dug a hole, so Kade laid her, wrapped in a blanket, into the ground and covered her up.

Maddie felt helpless. She followed Kade back to the barn, where he prepared formula for the two kids. She took a bottle from him and they sat down on the barn floor without anything being said. The baby goats nuzzled to the bottle and began feeding. It was exactly like having twin newborns only they didn't need to be burped. After the feeding, Kade brought in some lawn loungers and they sat and talked between feedings. Maggie didn't realize she'd fallen asleep until she heard voices. Wiping her eyes, she saw Kade standing by the barn door whispering to Rod.

"This isn't *Pet Sematary* from Stephen King," Rod mocked.

"I swear to you, Rod."

"You're also upset and sleep deprived, and, well, did you have anything to drink?" Rod pointed to a few glass bottles next to their makeshift baby goat nursery. "You were probably hallucinating, Kade."

Kade shook his head. "When have I ever made something up?"

"Let's go look then," Rod suggested, holding the door open wider so that the light danced in.

"Something I can help you with?" Maddie finally interrupted.

Kade and Rod looked surprised, as if forgetting that Maddie was even there.

Kade cleared his throat, but before he could answer Rod blurted out that Kade had seen Buffy come in and lay down with her babies. "He said she even fed them. Did you happen to see anything? Or smoke anything last night ...?"

Kade punched Rod in the arm.

"Ouch, that hurt, man."

"Maddie was sleeping. By the way, you snore loudly!"

Maddie blushed.

"I swear I saw what I saw. It wasn't the beer, and we had no drugs or hallucinogens. And yes, I'm sleep deprived, but ..." Kade combed his fingers through his hair. "Maybe she wasn't really dead."

Maddie worked in the intensive care unit. She'd seen denial before. It was a funny way grief played with the mind. Denial often dulls the shock of the loss, especially a sudden passing. She'd had many family members of patients swear they saw their loved one turn the corner of the hospital or asked to check for a pulse once more, positive that their loved one was still breathing. None of it was real at all, but it was very real to the grieving mind.

Rod held the door open for Maddie and Kade, and the three of them traipsed out to Buffy's grave. The ground was still undisturbed and there wasn't any sign of a Lazarus effect.

Kade looked dejected and embarrassed.

"Get some sleep," Rod said in a soft voice. "Maddie, there's a guest room, I suggest you do the same before driving home. I've got kid duty. Plus, some of the teenagers from the high school are coming over to help out."

Maddie felt as if she'd worn out her welcome and, instead of following Kade to his front porch, she headed to her car. Kade didn't notice until he turned to hold the door open for her, and instead saw her backing out of his long gravel driveway and head toward the highway.

"Well, I screwed that one up," he muttered under his voice to nobody in particular. "Mom always said that timing was important for real estate and love, and I guess I suck at the love part."

After taking a much-needed hot shower, Kade climbed into bed, but instead of closing his eyes, he grabbed his cell phone and clicked the power button. No texts. Of course there weren't texts, she's a sensible person and probably sleeping or still driving. Thinking for a moment, and never being someone who followed the love rules, which could be part of the problem, he sent Maddie a text that simply said, "Thanks for all your help. Coffee this weekend? I promise I'm not crazy." He hit send. *Oh my gosh, everybody that said they weren't crazy were probably crazy.* Quickly he sent another. "I'm not crazy like a real crazy person, just a goat-loving person." Again he hit send. And then he wondered if that sounded really crazy and contemplated sending another explaining that he was an animal lover, but not in a creepy way, but before he could second-guess himself anymore, he fell fast asleep.

His room was dark when he opened his eyes. There was some commotion downstairs, and he could hear Rod's voice. Even though he kept an open-door policy on his farm, it was rare for any of his staff to enter his home. Sliding out of bed, he opened the door and came face-to-face with Rod.

"You look like you've seen a ghost. What's up?"

"I think I've seen a ghost," Rod simply stated.

"You saw her too?" Kade whispered, astonished.

Rod nodded. "I was feeding the babes and felt like someone was watching me. There she was, standing by the end of the pen, just watching us. She turned around and disappeared."

It was that same afternoon that Kade called me.

"Kade, I've never tried to tune into a goat. I can give you a couple names and numbers of animal communicators," I offered.

"Honestly, Kristy, I think this is all nuts. I've never seen a goat ghost, so maybe this is a first for us both, but I saw her, Kristy. I saw Buffy."

It wasn't that I didn't like a challenge, I just had never purposely tried to tune into an animal on the Other Side. They've just appeared. And then there was a distance. He was in Minnesota and there was no way I was going to be able to travel there, but Kade was determined that I could assist him so we set up a Skype session for the next morning.

I was so worried that I would disappoint him that I barely slept. I kept talking to my guides and angels, begging them to make a goat appear and speak in the hopes of helping with answers. It doesn't quite work that way, though, as I'm quite aware.

When I give sessions, lectures, or events, I often give a spiel something like: When we connect to spirit we have to stay open. They don't work on the same vibrational path that we do. You may not always receive the messages that you want, but you will always receive the messages that you need, whether you see it now or not. It's a divine direction and information they offer that isn't necessarily gospel; it's their opinions and their beliefs, just as they had here on Earth. They have more insight, but we still have ego to work with. Often those who want to connect to their loved ones on the Other Side have an unrealistic notion that they will receive the meaning of life, the winning lottery ticket, or some other life-changing information. It doesn't mean that it can't happen, but it rarely happens.

So here I was ready to speak to Kade, who sounded like an intelligent man, who wanted to speak to a goat. I wasn't certain how this would go. I continued trying to remind myself that expectation was a recipe for disaster and to just go with the flow. The flow of a goat. I laughed at myself, but then I remembered my conversation with Rowa and how he said communication is communication whether human or animal, it's soul based. Taking a deep breath in and then out, I opened Skype and clicked on Kade's number, setting it for video conferencing.

Kade's blue eyes were intense as he listened to me explain how a session goes.

"I tune into your energy, calling on your guides, my guides, and any past loved ones, and they give me information that I pass along to you. I say to expect the unexpected and to not get frustrated if the information doesn't make sense at first. The Other Side has a better memory than we do, seeing as they are without the worldly weight that we all carry. Ready?"

Kade nodded.

I closed my eyes and turned on my intuitive switch, if you will. Standing there, in my mind's eye, was a tall, lanky man. He looked to be in his early eighties, although he had a head full of gray hair and a bushy mustache that was mostly black in color. He wore a plain gold wedding band, overalls with a red checkered flannel shirt, and work boots. His hands were large and callused. "What's your name?" I whispered to him clairvoyantly.

"I went by Slim," he answered. "But he'll know me as Gramps."

Slim didn't crack any emotion. He simply stood there as if he'd been uncomfortably summoned. I apologized to him if I was interrupting him, and he waved me off as if swatting a fly.

"Nonsense, this is my grandson and he's troubled," he snapped.

It was obviously his personality, and nothing to take personal, I realized.

"Have you by chance seen a goat cross over?" I asked, squinting like I was ready for someone to throw a ball in my face.

"I've got goats, horses, cats, dogs, sheep, and rabbits with me. I thought my farming days were over when I crossed over, but nope, I'm stuck with all of them." Slim offered a smile. "But I don't have to shovel manure or remember to feed them or pay for a blacksmith or anything. I get to enjoy them here."

I loved what Slim was sharing, but he wasn't answering my question, so I thought I'd be direct. "Slim, is there a goat named Buffy there with you?"

"Buffy is with Ma. Want me to get her for you?"

Before I could say anything, Slim disappeared. I wasn't certain if Slim was getting Buffy or Ma, but I hoped for both. I took the moment to fill Kade in.

"So Buffy isn't a ghost then?" Kade asked, confused.

"Not if she's crossed over and with your grandparents. She's more than likely just checking on her babies, and maybe you too," I suggested.

Slim, Ma, and Buffy appeared. Ma looked radiant with rosy cheeks and sparkling green eyes. She lovingly laid her hand on Buffy's head. Buffy responded by nuzzling back.

"Tell Kade it's time. It's time for him to sell the farm, or at least get more help. It's time for him to have a life. It's time for him to sell the baby goats. It's time," Ma said.

"No way," Kade responded when I repeated the message. "I promised to take care of that land. I can remember being at the kitchen table, I must've been eight years old, and I promised I would keep it together. Nobody else wanted it when Gramps died, and everyone said I was crazy. I keep promises. I have to."

Gramps scowled. "Yes, he keeps promises. We know that, but farming was my dream, not his. Buffy is trying to tell him to move on. Find a girl. Get married. Start a family. Do something he's excited about. This isn't it."

Ma nodded in agreement. "It's time."

"So that's why Buffy keeps visiting?" I asked.

"Buffy wants him to know that it wasn't his fault. She was ten years old. Well past her prime to have more kids. Those babies of hers, though, there's someone else they belong to and he needs to know that they can go."

Kade looked upset. "But I made a promise," he whispered.

"Ma also says that there's a girl you just met. She's the one. Don't mess it up."

"She said that?" Kade laughed. "Yeah, that sounds like Ma. I think I already messed it up, though."

"Tell him we love him and we are proud of him. He'll know what to do, and when, with the farm, the animals, and the girl," Ma said.

"Goats are an interesting animal guide," I told Kade. "The goat reminds us that we can make promises, but they aren't worth anything if we don't honor our own ideas and dreams. We have to be good to ourselves, too. You don't get rewarded unless you take some risks. And goats, well, they like to explore and climb, and beat the odds—it's a great message for you to take on too, per your grandparents along with Buffy. Embrace uncertainty. Some of the most beautiful chapters don't have a title until much later."

Kade thanked me for the session, although I think it left us both a bit confused. I was also disappointed Buffy never spoke to me, she spoke through Kade's grandparents to me, and maybe that was okay.

A month later Kade sent me a message.

Kristy,

I'm sorry that I didn't message earlier. Life has been a bit chaotic, but I wanted to fill you in. The day after our reading, a friend of my grandparents' showed up at the farm and asked if I was willing to sell a portion of the land, along with the animals. I was confused and hurt and in awe all at the same time. I signed over the paperwork yesterday, and, get this, the farm will be used to help children with different disabilities and they are even going to create a camp. I still have the house, a couple acres, and a small stake in the farm, and all my staff gets to stay on. It was a win-win situation.

Also, that girl that Ma talked about—we are dating and taking things slow, but I do believe she's the one, and she has embraced the craziness of everything over the past month.

I haven't seen Buffy since, so I'm hoping she likes the changes and is happy that her kids are doing great and growing.

Thanks again, Kristy, but you probably already know all of this, right?

Kade wasn't living his dream, and it seemed even Buffy, his goat, knew it. Our pets don't want their passing to bring so much pain, neither do our human loved ones who've crossed over. They want you to instead remember them as happy and pain free. Visits from the Other Side are rarely a message to put you on high alert, instead they are simply letting you know that they are okay and want you to be okay too.

It's easy to see why Kade thought Buffy was a ghost. You see people in life who just seem to have it together. They are filled with good energy. They smile. They get up when they fall down. They understand how to play the game of life. Then you see people in life who just seem to never get it together. They play the victim or become the victim. They are the ones always miserable, I call them the Eeyores of life, and it is always someone else's fault. They are sometimes even called psychic vampires or takers, and they will try and convince you that you are insecure if you aren't constantly allowing them to feed off of you.

Those who seem to get life seem to get death, and cross over with ease and become a spirit. Often those who didn't get life, don't cross over for any amount of reasons, including being afraid of judgment or wanting someone else to do the work for them, even on the Other Side. They stay earthbound as a ghost, until they cross over. There's the exception, however. There's the unexpected or tragic passing that can leave a spirit in shock, until they recognize what happened and either make the walk to the Other Side or just plain won't accept that they've passed away. Sometimes there's unfinished business, and this is often portrayed by Hollywood as the angry ghost throwing objects, scratching people, and opening and closing cupboards and drawers. It can happen, but it's not as common as television shows and movies make it out to be.

Ghosts can and do travel. They aren't stuck to a particular room in a building, an object, or land space. Spirits on the Other Side travel as well; they are lighter, without as much emotional baggage. So ghosts are the ones with the heavy luggage, and spirits have none or maybe just a carry on.

This becomes fuzzy with animals (no pun intended) because they rarely have the emotional baggage. This makes it easier for them to be beside you, if you allow them to be. The spirit world and physical world coexist, and although they don't have their flesh, blood, or fur, they still remain intact, with their mannerisms, personality, and love.

When our boundaries are unguarded or unclear, we set ourselves up for sadness. It's more than okay to create strong boundaries. It's more than okay to say *no* to what doesn't bring you peace. Opinions are a dime a dozen, and loyalty isn't just a word—it's so much more. If you feel disconnected to your life purpose, ask your pets on the Other Side for help. They wanted you to be happy when they were here, and they want to see you happy with them on the Other Side.

～ 7 ～

HEARING THE OTHER SIDE

Old Sam was born on April 4, 1849, at the Abraham C. Fisk Breeding Stables in Coldwater Michigan. Before the Civil War, his job was to pull a streetcar back and forth, carrying passengers from the train station to the hotel that was owned by Cyrus Orlando Loomis, whose father managed the hotel.

Cyrus was selected to be the commander of the volunteer artillery of Michigan, later known as Loomis Battery. As the war continued on, so did the accumulations of bodies of both soldiers and their horses. More of both were in demand, and the Loomis Battery was asked for donations of horses. Old Sam was now twelve years old, and while most of the war horses were three to five years of age, he was one of two hundred donated horses. After rigorous training at Fort Wayne in Detroit, the horses were sent off to battle, and Sam marched into the brutal Battle of Rich Mountain, in the area we now call West Virginia. Old Sam continued his grueling battle duties for four long years afterward. He stood strong and proud through the hardship and fatigue of the war and became a favorite among the men that he fought along with, who treated him with love and respect as if he was human. In the end, Sam would be the only survivor of all the two hundred horses donated.

His homecoming was met with a bittersweet celebration. Although he returned, 199 other horses didn't, along with 40 of his human comrades. Sam had been wounded several times and half starved, but he was a fighter and the townsfolk knew it, and through their sadness they still whistled and cheered for him, giving him a hero's welcome.

Upon exiting the train, Old Sam trotted down the street as if it was a parade made just for him. He instantly recognized his surroundings and leisurely walked to the hotel, his home, and right to his stall. The witnesses were in awe, but they were also struck by the tenacity of the horse. The owner of the hotel decided right then that Old Sam would not have to work another day of his life, and he would see green pastures and only be a carriage horse if he wanted.

The war was now part of Old Sam's soul, and he was often led around town for parades and war reunions. A bronze plaque telling Old Sam's story was mounted in the town square, and he had his own plaque alongside his human comrades, honoring him as a war veteran. So when he passed away on November 8, 1876, at twenty-seven years old, news carried far, and a petition that he be buried in Oak Grove Cemetery next to the other veterans was called out. It was illegal to bury an animal in a human cemetery in Michigan, though. So when the sexton of the cemetery decided to take an emergency trip out of town, he loudly let everyone know his departure and return dates and times. A plot to bury Old Sam in an unmarked grave was immediately crafted.

So in the dead of night, the town buried Old Sam in the illegal grave for his forever rest, covering it with fallen leaves, but giving him military honors as well. Today in Oak Grove Cemetery, Old Sam has a monument marker with an American Flag denoting his rich hero history. Although his body lay in the old cemetery up on the hill, his soul and spirit are said to still visit the town of Coldwater, Michigan.

More than mere legend, you will find most all of the Coldwater residents have a story or two about hearing Old Sam trot down the street. Jill, a lifelong resident of Coldwater, had heard the stories of Old Sam as a child, thinking nothing of it but old history. I was doing a ghost hunt in the town when Jill asked if she could share her story.

"I had just graduated high school and taken the job of a babysitter. It was late at night and I had heard the train whistle blow. That in itself wasn't unusual, but just a minute or two afterward I heard the trot of a horse clip-clop down the street. I was sure someone was playing a trick on me, you know, trying to scare me or something. The kids and I went out on the front porch, and so did everyone else on the block. We couldn't see anything, but we heard Old Sam walk by our homes, giving a neigh every so often, until the hoof sounds quieted as he got farther and farther down the street and disappeared as it got closer to the cemetery. Then nothing," Jill shared. She took a deep breath and began again, "My last experience with Old Sam was just a few years back. I was divorcing and going through a rough time. Oddly enough, cemeteries bring me peace, so I went for a walk in Oak Grove."

Jill's voice caught and tears began to roll down her cheek. "Honestly, I was going to ... end my life there," she confessed.

I handed her a tissue and a bottle of water and told her to take her time. It was apparent that her soul and spirit were still healing from past scars. Jill quickly gained composure, sat straighter and began again, "I had a bottle of pills and was going to lay my head down on my mom's stone and join her. I know, stupid, but at the time it sounded like the best plan. But just as I sat down on the hard ground, I heard a noise of the clattering of hooves on concrete, and looked up to see … not exactly a clear figure, but the figure of a horse and a rider. I know it sounds absurd." Jill laughed at the memory.

I smiled at her with the reassurance that I found it anything but absurd.

"I hadn't taken any pills, and I'd only been drinking straight water that day, so I was clearheaded except for my emotional despair. The rider jumped off the horse, stood next to me, and spoke!"

"He spoke?" I exclaimed.

Although many have experiences with the Other Side, not many have an encounter that involves actually speaking, as it takes a lot of energy for a spirit to emulate words. Instead, many describe their encounters as a feeling or hearing a voice inside their head or smelling something, but rarely the spoken word.

Jill nodded. "Yes, he spoke. He said he was sorry I had lost faith in myself, but he saw a light that wasn't to be extinguished. He then patted his horse on the head, got back on, and called out for Old Sam to continue on. He called him by name. I watched as the man jumped on the horse and then I lost them to shadows behind the trees. The man and his horse saved my life."

Jill's recollection of a visit from Old Sam is one of many experiences those in and around Coldwater have had. Maybe not as life changing as her own, but significant nonetheless. Jill believed it was the spirit of Cyrus who rode Sam around the town. Or maybe it was Sam riding Cyrus around town, reminding others that we all have a war to fight. Some even feel like they are on the front lines, but that the war can be won with determination and bravery. A horse doesn't look backward. It if did, it might stumble and fall. Jill decided to use her ghostly visit from Old Sam to help others with the lessons she learned.

"It's not a story I always share," she confessed. "I hope he's not disappointed in that."

I'm betting he's not worried about the accolades, but the sentiment. Jill's life mission since then has been in the mental illness field, specific to suicide prevention. She bought a farm not far from Old Sam's home and use horses as a form of therapy. I'm sure that Old Sam and Cyrus are very proud.

MEOW

"Meow's health began to deteriorate when she turned twelve, but she continued to keep her ritual of wanting her treats in the morning, and if you weren't there before 7 a.m., she'd jump on the bed to make sure you woke up with a huge meow. Just one." Natalie smiled. "She was never a very vocal cat.

"It was a holiday, and I didn't need to get the kids up for school, so I decided to turn off the alarm clock and sleep in, but, sure enough, Meow was on top of me, waking me up at 7:30. Not at all happy, I pulled the covers over my head, hoping she'd just lay down and fall asleep, but she kept meowing, one after the other after the other until I got up. As soon as I got up, though, I saw Meow's body, cold and rigid, on the floor by the bedroom door. She must've passed during the night."

Meow continues to visit Natalie and the kids every so often with her one meow, always in the early morning.

SAVED BY THE BELL

The kennel planned to euthanize the seven-week-old golden retriever puppies, as they were all ill, but an organization came in the nick of time and rescued them. Without a mom to nurse them, the head of the rescue tirelessly cared for the sick pups, lovingly feeding them with an eye dropper until they got bigger and stronger. Each one of them survived, and at ten weeks they were ready to be adopted.

Janis and her family had first dibs to look at the pups, and therefore was given first pick. They all sat down on the ground and watched each of the rambunctious puppies run around, trying to decipher which puppy would become their puppy. There was one that stood out. Instead of running around in circles with her siblings, she sat quietly and watched the commotion from the sidelines. Janis's husband teasingly swooped up the pup and placed her in his shirt pocket, where she contently sat. It was love at first sight. They named her Hannah. With her already rough start in life, she was frightened, and for several days she refused to leave the couch, having to be handfed and cuddled with all night long. After four days, she finally climbed off the couch and found her way into the home and hearts of her forever family.

Hannah found her confidence and readily took on the responsibility of being a foster mom to whatever puppies needed her. When the family brought home Halle, a West Highland terrier, she was ecstatic. Unfortunately, Janis wasn't because Halle decided that potty training wasn't for her.

"I finally told Hannah that if she wanted Halle to stay she had to potty train her. As if she understood me, and obviously she did, Hannah began to take Halle outside and show her what to do, despite all of us trying and failing. Halle never messed in my house after that," Janis shared.

Hannah and Halle became instant friends and they did everything together from then on.

Janis's husband's job was transferring them from Michigan to Florida, and they needed to get things settled before bringing the dogs with them, so Halle and Hannah went to stay with Janis's parents. They had stayed before and enjoyed their time with their grandparents, so Janis was wasn't concerned until the dogs were being dropped off. Hannah communicated a look of sadness and a final good-bye with her eyes. She was aging, and Janis hoped that she was overanalyzing it, but she held Hannah tighter, kissed her, and told her she loved her a dozen times before leaving. Hannah licked Janis's face and pushed into her shoulders as if to offer her own hug and cuddle.

They left the next morning for Florida, but three days later they got a call notifying them that Hannah was not doing well. She was having a hard time walking, was not eating, and could not stand for any length of time. All they wanted to do was run for the airport, but there were other responsibilities and commitments that needed to be completed and that just wasn't feasible. Janis's brother took Hannah to the veterinarian and it was decided that Hannah was in pain and would not live much longer, and so over the phone they had to make a very hard decision to let her go.

Janis and her husband hadn't even unpacked from their trip when they went to the veterinarian to pick up Hannah's ashes. They were in a beautiful box the same color as her hair. They also had a clay paw print made and her collar that had her license and name tag that would clang together when Hannah would shake her head.

Halle, the Westie, was obviously depressed and sad by the loss of her best friend, but when they made their move to Naples, Florida, she found some new spunk. One of the first things that Janis unpacked was Hannah's cremated remains, the cast of her paw print, and her collar, and she placed them on a bookcase in the library of their home.

One night at about 10 p.m., they were spending some quiet time reading. Halle was sleeping next to the chair Janis was sitting in. Janis and her husband were just about to go to bed when there was a distinct sound of Hannah shaking her collar. They'd heard that sound for fourteen years and were taken aback. Halle ran to the bookshelf, looked up at the collar, and began to bark excitedly, as if welcoming home her old friend.

"We had been talking about her so often since she passed, and both my husband and I have felt so guilty for not being with her when she died. I got goose bumps that night, but I also felt so happy because I really felt comforted to know that she was with us." Janis smiled at the memory.

It happened again, though. Janis couldn't sleep, so she got out of bed at 5 a.m. and went into the library to read. Halle was in the bedroom with her husband when Janis heard the collar jingle. Thinking Halle was up and wanted to go out, she got up only to see the bedroom door was closed. When she opened the door, Halle was snoring away.

Janis knew that it was Hannah and blew her a kiss.

Animals on the Other Side are able to interact with animals still here, just as human souls can interact with human and animals here. Animals on the physical plane are able to see and interact with those who have passed often clearer than humans.

GETTING PAST GUILT

When you can recognize that your pet isn't gone, is when you can release the guilt you feel.

THREE LEGS ARE BETTER THAN FOUR

When a client posted on her Facebook page that she found a litter of kittens in a wishing well on her sister's property, along with a photo of the kittens, I melted. All snuggled together were several kittens all different colors, but it was the little orange kitten that made my heart skip a beat, and I replied in jest that I needed that one.

"Kristy, the orange kitten only has three legs," she informed me.

And my heart melted even more.

I decided to share the photo in hopes of finding homes or a rescue for the kittens, but my mind couldn't stop thinking of that little orange face. An acquaintance who works at a local rescue saw my posting and sent me a warning that if anyone got a hold of the three legged one they would more than likely just put that kitten down. It only took me a minute before I bounced the idea of saving the kitten to my husband Chuck and my kids.

"We will just take the kitten until I can find a suitable home for him or her," I leveraged.

After all, we already had a menagerie of animals at our home. Some can call it a sanctuary, others might call it animal hoarding. I call it insanity.

And they all agreed that we had to save the kitten.

"We aren't naming him," I warned.

Chuck just smirked at me and the kids gave one another knowing looks.

"What? I mean it," I said, only to hear them all laugh at me.

My dad lives with us (or I live with him, depending upon who you talk to), and although I'm an adult and can make decisions, there's something about wanting the acceptance of a parent. Then there's just not telling him and making a decision and praying he doesn't yell and scream.

A week after the Facebook posting, we picked up the kitten, and I fell in love the moment he snuggled in my arms. His blue-green eyes looked at us lovingly and oh so trusting on the ride home. He enjoyed his chin and belly rubs and didn't miss a purr.

"What's his name?" my daughter Micaela asked me from the back seat, grinning.

"Captain Archibald," I said, not missing a beat. "He fought a tough battle for that tuna on the seven seas," I teased.

As we introduced Archie to the other animals, they looked at him as just another addition to the family and not as disabled at all. He walked and ran with a different gait, but nobody much care. The other cats and dogs chased him as much as they did their other brothers and sister, bathed him just the same as the others, and fought with him without caring that he had three legs.

"Who is this?" my dad asked when he saw the new addition.

I started to ramble, explaining that I would find him a home once I got him fixed up and he was a bit older, continuing to make excuses. My dad just laughed.

"He's obviously ours." he smiled, picking up the orange tabby and snuggling him in his arms. "A misfit like the rest of us."

Archie went through an amputation of most all of the remainder of the leg and sometimes has some phantom pain. Most of the time he doesn't realize that the leg isn't there and he tries to itch with it, so he requires extra help bathing (which the other animals assist with), ear cleaning, and petting, but he's healthy and happy. He doesn't sit around moping about his situation. He runs, jumps, eats, and loves without excuses because there's no such thing as a disability to him.

Accidents Happen

I've had clients who lost their beloved dog from drowning, another had a dog that jumped a fence and her collar got caught on the wire, and another where her husband accidently backed over her cat of just a year. Birds have flown away. Pet snakes, hamsters, guinea pigs, and turtles have escaped, never to return. Horses have had freak accidents, and potbelly pigs have eaten the wrong thing and died. Guilt is a normal reaction, and it's part of grieving. The only thing you can do that is heathy with that guilt is learn from it, most importantly learn how to forgive others and yourself.

After introductions, my first client, June, told me that she followed me on social media and had loved all the statuses about Archie. When I began the session, I always ask everyone to take a deep breath in and say their full name and birth date out loud. This is my way of dialing the phone to the Other Side and it helps invite the client's loved ones to come forward with their messages. As soon as June said her name, several people stepped forward, but it was her mom who stood in front of everyone, and she was holding a cat.

"June, your mom stands here. She says she had Alzheimer's and that you took her in, and when she was passing you never left her side. She's so thankful for all you did for her. She says that she wasn't easy to be with and she made a lot of mistakes, and she hopes you will forgive her."

June was mute, staring at me.

"She's also holding a cat," I added. Squinting to see if I could make out any details, I continued, "A very large and fuzzy black cat with some white color on his paws."

June bit her lower lip before she spoke. "Maybe it's my grandma, Kristy. Or Dad. I always think Dad is probably caring for my cat."

The lady shook her head in disagreement. "No, I'm her mom. I promise. She has my middle name."

I shared the message, which fell on deaf ears. I wasn't impressing her, but before I could get too frustrated June's dad came through. His energy was calm and gentle.

"Ma hated animals. She's confused because she's holding her cat," he informed me.

"Why are you holding her cat?" I curiously asked her mom.

"I grew up on a farm," her mom explained to me, ignoring my direct question. "Animals were things and my dad, her grandfather, wouldn't allow us to get close to them. The pigs got slaughtered. The cows were money and not something to be loved. The cats were to take care of the rodents. The dogs were to herd the animals. Animals weren't for companionship; they were to work and to give us a roof over our head."

Of course most kids are natural animal lovers, and June was no exception. When a neighbor had a litter of kittens when she was all of eight years old, she carefully chose a petite calico and brought it home. Her mom, Lola, wasn't amused and screamed for her to take it immediately back. Filthy animals didn't belong in the house and there would never ever be any type of animal in *their* house. Hurt and heartbroken, June returned the kitten, but it didn't stop her love for animals, and she loved visiting her friends' homes, where some had turtles, cats, dogs, rabbits, ferrets, and so on.

When she announced upon high school graduation that she was going to be a veterinarian, the response from her mom was the same as when she was eight years old. Her mom threatened to pull her college money and inheritance if she continued to pursue a *ridiculous dream*. So June, defeated, chose instead to major in business. After graduation, she took a job out of her home state of Michigan and, before even buying furniture for her new home, she went to a rescue and chose a small black kitten with white paws. She named him Figaro. He was loving, and healthy, except that he was born with only three legs. When her mother found out about the cat, they didn't speak for more than a year. That was until June's dad suddenly passed away and Lola needed help. So June moved back home, with Figaro in tow.

"Fig would jump in her lap and she'd scream and push him off." June laughed for just one beat. "Fig didn't care, though, and continued to try and win her over. It wasn't until she got Alzheimer's when she allowed him in her lap. In fact, I was a bit jealous for a bit because Fig took to sleeping with Ma instead of me. As her Alzheimer's worsened, Fig spent more and more time snuggling with her. It was when I saw her crying and holding him in her arms that it really touched me," June said, wiping her eyes.

I handed her a bottled water, allowing her to take a drink and collect herself.

June opened her purse and dug to the bottom while Lola stood tense, obviously not the type to allow her emotions to show. Her energy, though, filled the room with regret.

"You think she stole time from you?" I pressed.

June looked everywhere but at me, fiddling with the cap on her water bottle.

"When I died," Lola's spirit began again, "I took Fig with me. It wasn't my fault, though."

I was given an image of an urn filled with Lola's ashes next to an urn with Fig's name on it, but it was empty. Then they showed me the open door.

Lola passed away at home with June and hospice by her side. When the funeral home took her body, though, somehow the door wasn't latched shut and Figaro got out.

"I put flyers everywhere," June said as she nervously picked at her cuticles. "I checked animal shelters, and posted all over the web. I spent days and nights driving around. I prayed. I put cat food outside. I put litter outside. I did everything that everyone told me to do, but he never came home." June held tight to a bright red collar with silver tags. "He'd never gotten out before, and with three legs you wouldn't think he'd get far."

I gave her a sympathetic smile. My own Archie could race up the stairs faster than his counterparts that had all fours.

"I made her take that collar off of him because it kept me awake," Lola said. She lovingly squeezed the spirit of Fig. "Maybe if it was on, someone would've found him and called."

"Did he suffer, Kristy? Do you think I'm a horrible person for not caring how my mother is? All I want to know is if Fig forgives me—if he still loves me."

I was given an image that Fig found his way into someone's garage and simply passed away not long after he went missing. Some say that animals have an instinct to run away when they are going to die. Those on the Other Side have given me a bit of a cynical view on that. It's not that they don't want you to see them pass, but instead it could be they became disoriented. They might've had a hearing or eye issue and can't find their way back, they were hit by a car, or they were attacked by an animal. It's rare for them to just wander off. The feeling that I got off of Fig was that he had a case of senior dementia that wasn't seen because Lola's health issues were the main focus. Fig willed himself to pass after he lost his way.

"I felt as though I was falling into an abyss of depression."

I gave June a telling look.

"Yes, I'm horribly guilty," June admitted. "I'm still in the abyss."

June had nothing to feel guilty about. She was hurt, confused, mad, and grieving. Death without closure, whether a human companion or an animal companion, is difficult. June didn't have the closure.

"Figaro is right there. So is your mom, whether you want her here or not," I told June. "I'd like you to ask for Figaro's forgiveness."

"That's just silly," she quickly snapped.

"Why? Because you don't believe Fig is here or because you have nothing to be forgiven for?"

June hung her head in silence.

"Your mom says that you had a dream, well, what I would call a visit, soon after their passing."

Instead of answering me, June's buried emotions became unleased. "I'm so angry, Kristy. I wasn't allowed pets growing up and now my mom has my cat with her! How is that fair? How dare she?"

I was taught life wasn't fair, and that everything happens for a reason, we just didn't know all of the reasons. I didn't buy into either sentiment, but I didn't have an answer for her.

In the movie *Ghost* with Patrick Swayze, Whoopi Goldberg's character channels his ghost. It's something I've done a few times, but I never liked it. Being a control freak means having a spirit enter into me and speak through me just feels dirty, so I was surprised when I felt as if I was having an out-of-body experience. I didn't feel myself talking, but I was hearing myself speak, only it wasn't me.

"In your visit, Fig was running through a bright green field of grass. He had all four of his legs, and he was happy. And then your mom told you not to worry, that he was being taken care of and would always be yours. She also told you that although there was no such thing as a replacement, the only way for you to heal was to go to the shelter. You'd know who belonged to you and who you belonged to, but you haven't done that."

June's eyes were wide, and she sat on the edge of her chair, deciding whether or not to bolt.

The other thing with channeling is that it exhausts me, and so just as quickly as I wasn't me, I was back to me, only like I'd just ran a couple miles. June's wide eyes matched mine.

"I'm so sorry," I said. "I don't know ..."

"You sounded just like my mother for a second." June looked at me crooked.

"Well, was she right?"

June nodded.

"Let's work on getting past this guilt, okay?"

Sometimes there's no basis for guilt, but it's a normal response, nonetheless. Our pets rely on us, and when we can't protect them we can feel like a failure. It's so easy to isolate yourself, even tell yourself that you'll never get another pet. The cost of love is high, but it is well worth it.

June decided to commit to journaling. Some days it was just a thought, others it was chapters. Through her journaling, she realized she wanted to volunteer at an animal shelter. It was her way of helping, staying busy, but also getting more social.

The Christmas card June sent me the next year made me smile. The enclosed picture showed her holding a large orange cat that could've been my Archie's sister.

"This is Lola. No, I didn't name her, she was already named. Oddly enough I think she looks a bit like my mom too with her bright orange hair, but don't tell her that I think that. I knew immediately she was mine. Thanks, Kristy. Not only do I know that our pets go to Heaven, and they are whole and healed, I know that I can be whole and healed on Earth too by allowing to love and be loved."

Figaro wasn't forgotten, she just realized she had more than enough love to share.

RAIN DROP

I was hired at a restaurant a bit over an hour away from home to host a Halloween event. In the middle of dinner, the bartender pulled me aside to take a phone call. It was my dad. His Shih Tzu, Rain Drop, had just died.

"I gave him a piece of roast beef and then he died. Maybe he choked on it. Maybe I gave him too big of a slice," he lamented.

I was in the middle of the event and couldn't leave until the end, but the whole time I couldn't help but think of my dad's anguish.

When Chuck and I walked in that night, my dad had Rain's body next to him on the couch, snuggled in a blanket. His body was cold and stiff. Without any words, Chuck picked up Rain, took him outside, and buried him in the wildflower garden. For months, my dad brought up that night, rewinding it to see what he might've done wrong. He continued to question himself until we went to the veterinarian with his other dog and he shared with her what had happened.

"Ron," the vet looked at him sympathetically and said, "I don't think he choked, it sounds like he just had a heart attack and died."

"You think so?" My dad looked at her, not sure if she was simply trying to make him feel better.

She nodded. "Had he been coughing a lot before then?"

"Yes. A lot, actually. Almost like he was clearing his throat."

The veterinarian put her hand on my dad's shoulder. "It was congestive heart failure, and there was nothing you could've done. He died eating a piece of roast, which to him was probably heavenly."

Although I think it made my dad feel better to hear that he wasn't responsible, I'm not sure he completely bought it.

Rain was notorious for barking at everything and anything. It drove us crazy, but especially my husband. Not long after Rain's passing our neighbor brought home a puppy, and we would find the next-door neighbor's puppy run to the spot where Rain's body was and bark uncontrollably, as if channeling Rain to spite Chuck.

SAMSON

Samson was a gorgeous full-bred German shepherd, but when I brought him home my then father-in-law joked that there wasn't any way he was all German shepherd and that he was either part beagle or dachshund. Samson had the droopiest and longest ears for his breed, but it wasn't long that he grew into them. He was a handsome tricolor, and he resembled a typical police dog. Although his bark was big, he was gentle, loving, and obedient. Not everyone likes German shepherds, though. They feel threatened, as was the case with one of our neighbors who would always ask if I was certain he wouldn't bite. Samson never attempted to bite, even when playing rough, so I was confused as to why he was even asking.

We'd let Samson and our other dog out and soon after called them to come back in, but one day Samson didn't come back. That's when I saw him. He lay on the ground, in the middle of the yard, dead. I ran him to the emergency vet, who told me that they could do an autopsy, but it was costly. Being young and mostly broke, I couldn't afford that. The doctor told me it was either poisoning or a heart attack. The neighbor never asked what happened to Samson or ever looked me in the eye after his death, which made me wonder if he'd fed him something, poisoning him. For years I felt guilty. I felt guilty for not protecting him. I felt guilty for not getting the autopsy. I felt guilty for not standing up to the neighbor. I felt guilty. Then I had a dream where Samson was sitting next to my bed, handsome as ever. There was no anger or disappointment in his eyes, there was only love.

LOVESTOCK

Gordie came up to me after a library event that I was speaking at. He was a bit shy and reserved, and I could tell it took a lot of courage for him to talk to me. I pulled him away from the crowd at the table to see if that helped, but as soon as I touched his shoulder my hand felt hot, like it was touching a hot iron.

"Do animals forgive?" he asked me, without a backstory.

"I don't believe animals hold grudges like humans do," I answered, still feeling the heat on my hand. "Often times, though, we are our own worst enemies and no forgiveness from another is really needed, except within ourselves."

Gordie thought about that for a moment and asked me to repeat it.

"Whatever you feel guilty for, you have to let that go," I reworded.

"It was a freak accident. The barn was locked up for the night and all my animals died in a fire." Gordie bent his head down and gulped back a sob. "I tried to get them, but I couldn't. I burned my hands, and I couldn't even feel it. I didn't even care. I was supposed to take care of them. They relied on me to take care of them."

Gordie grabbed me in a hug, sobbing on my shoulder.

I couldn't imagine his anguish, but I certainly felt it. "They knew you loved them and you will see them again one day, but your job isn't to punish yourself anymore."

"How do I get over this?" he asked me, pitifully.

I wished I had all the answers, but everyone grieves differently and every loss is unique. There's no one size fits all about death. I suggested that he create a monument for his lost animals, maybe next to the rebuilt barn. A token of love, not a constant remembrance of grief.

"I don't know if I can ever ride again," he confessed.

But in my mind's eye I saw a rebuilt barn filled with animals. Riding again for him meant loving again. It's so much easier to pretend you'll never love again, allowing yourself to suffer for an accident that isn't yours to punish yourself for.

Gordie did rebuild two years later, and he reopened his farm with a menagerie of animals from rabbits to sheep and, of course, horses. He decided to make it a place where kids could come and learn about life, death, grief, and love, and he named it LoveStock.

If you are feeling guilty about your pet's passing, stop the thought pattern by recognizing the thought and turning off your negative mental chat that could be sabotaging the life that you so deserve. How do you do that? The first thing is by acknowledging that you are doing it and when a negative thought arises, tell yourself STOP! (preferably out loud) and then replace the negative thought with a positive one or a positive memory. Or simply take some deep breaths. We can't always have a head full of sunshine, but little by little you will notice that your negative thoughts will start to dissipate. Think of it as mental scum and you are erasing it away with your happy thoughts. Always remember that what you focus on expands, and if it is negative, then that is what you will get, and your pet on the Other Side won't want you to walk around gloomy and sad.

9

ADD MORE LOVE
TO YOUR HEART

It's easy to love, not so easy to lose, until you lose and then loving again is plain scary. Your pet doesn't want you to stop loving, though, because of your grief for them. There's a price for loving, but an even bigger price for not.

Dwight wasn't ready, but it seemed that his longtime best friend Kat was. Fifteen years ago, he'd gone to his local farmer's market to get tomatoes for his wife, Sharon, and came home with a six-week-old golden retriever. He forgot all about the tomatoes, so he wasn't sure what his wife was more upset about. It was love at first sight, though, and Kat was an amazing dog. She never once made any mistakes in the house and never chewed anything up either.

Time can be unforgiving to even animals, though, and after Sharon passed away from a brave battle of breast cancer, Kat's own health began to deteriorate. Dwight thought perhaps Kat had absorbed his own grief, but that would just be ego. Of course, Kat was grieving herself, of that he knew. When the funeral home took

Sharon's body, Kat followed them right out the door to the hearse. It took a lot of convincing to get her back in the house, and when he did, she jumped up in bed where Sharon had laid for several months and she whined. For the next couple months, Kat would run to look out the window, waiting for her to come home from her chemotherapy appointments. Only she never came home. She was a mile down the road at the local cemetery, in a plot next to their only child, a son who'd died of leukemia when he was just four years old.

The drive to the veterinarian was emotional, as you might imagine. All Dwight wanted to do was turn around and make all the hurt go away. He wanted his wife back. He wanted his son back. He wanted his dog back. He laughed for a brief moment as he remembered the old joke that when you played country music backward you got all that you lost back. *Too bad it didn't work*, he thought. He'd be all over that.

"Now remember, you have to go find Mom," he said to Kat, who looked at him with knowing eyes. "Give her a big hug for me and tell her how much I love and miss her."

Dwight wiped his eyes with the back of his hand and stroked the top of Kat's head.

The drive to Dr. Seagram's seemed so much shorter than he remembered. He sat in the parking lot shivering with emotion, even though it was more than 80 degrees outside. He never realized how many decisions Sue made until he didn't have her around to make them.

Dwight took a deep breath, hoping to inhale some confidence, and ushered Kat out of the car. She never needed a collar or a leash, keeping close to his side from early on, even without any training, so when Kat ran toward another car that had just parked, he thought it was unusual.

Maybe she's trying to escape, he wondered.

"Hi, there," a woman smiled, getting out of her car.

"I'm so very sorry," Dwight apologized and called for Kat to come, only she refused to budge. Instead, she sat in front of the stranger, nuzzling her hand for more pets. The stranger readily obliged.

"You are handsome," the woman gushed.

"She's a girl."

"Oh, sorry. You are a pretty girl," the lady corrected, patting Kat on the head.

"Thanks," Dwight answered back gruffly. He knew he sounded short, but he wanted their last moments of time to be his and his alone.

Dwight patted his right leg for Kat to come, but instead she followed the lady into the building, leaving Dwight behind.

Dr. Seagram was at the reception desk and offered a big smile when Dwight came in. "I see you've met my mom. Dwight, this is Betty Sue. And Mom, this is Dwight and that pretty lady there is Kat, my favorite patient. Just don't tell anyone else." Dr. Seagram smiled, holding her finger up in a hush.

"So Kat isn't feeling well?" the doctor asked, opening the door to the examining room and letting them both in, following right after. Before she closed the door, she called out, "Oh, Mom, can you catch the phones for me if they ring?"

"Sure thing, Beth. I mean, Dr. Seagram." Betty Sue smiled proudly, put her purse next to the desk, and took a seat.

"I think it's time, doctor," Dwight sniffled. "She's not been peppy, and she urinated in the house yesterday. She's never ever made any mistakes. Ever. She probably wants to be with her mom," he said in a self-defeated tone.

Dr. Seagram looked hard at Dwight before sitting on the floor with Kat. She touched the dog's tummy, and Kat winced in pain and then gave her a huge sloppy kiss on the face as if to apologize. Dwight and Dr. Seagram both chuckled.

"Dwight, I think Kat just has a urinary tract infection, and I can treat that with antibiotics. Now, it's up to you as to what you want to do. My professional opinion, though ..." Dr. Seagram hesitated, trying to make certain what she said came out gentle and understanding.

Dwight looked up at the veterinarian, knowing what was coming already. He'd heard it from several people, but hearing it and doing it were two different things.

Dr. Seagram continued, "My professional opinion is that you are so full of grief from Sharon that you are waiting for something else awful to happen and almost forcing away those who love you. Including Kat. You are allowed to be sad and grieve. Kat is allowed to be sad and grieve." Dr. Seagram touched Dwight's hand. "I think Kat's got a couple more years in her, though, but only if you start to take care of yourself. I think she's worried about you."

Dwight nodded and put his head down, staring in his lap.

"Let me give you a minute to think about it, okay?"

The doctor stepped out of the examine room and left Kat licking Dwight's face.

"Is everything okay, Beth?" her mom asked, noticing her daughter's energy shift.

Beth nodded. "I hope so," she said. As if a lightning strike hit her, she got an idea, but first had to wait for Dwight's decision.

Within seconds, the examine room door opened and Dwight walked out with Kat by his side.

"Let's try the antibiotics," Dwight said.

"Perfect," Dr. Seagram said. "What I'd like to do is keep her overnight and give her some extra fluids and the medicine intravenous, which should hopefully jump-start her healing. You can pick her up tomorrow, anytime after noon."

Dwight started to interject, but Beth cut him off. "I promise I won't keep her in a cage. She's my last patient, and only patient, so she can stay with me as I get caught up around here." Beth turned to her mom and said, "I'm sorry, I know we had lunch plans. Reservations are made and it'd be a waste for them to not be used. I think you and Dwight should go enjoy that sunshine. We'll do something tomorrow night, okay?"

Both Dwight and Betty Sue looked confused, but Beth wasted no time in pushing them both out the door with directions to the restaurant.

"My daughter can be pushy," Betty Sue apologized. "The dinner is paid for, though, and it'd be a waste to not go and enjoy it."

"I'm hungry too, so okay," Dwight mumbled, still mystified as to what just happened. "I think I know where the restaurant is. Do you want to follow me or I can drive?"

"I'm staying with Beth," Betty Sue said, pointing to a house in back of the animal clinic that Dwight had never noticed before. "Maybe you can drive and then check on Kat when we get back?"

Dwight nodded and opened the passenger door for Betty Sue to get in. As much as Sharon used to tell him it was the twenty-first century and that she could open and close her own door, it was something Dwight had always done. But never for another woman. It felt odd.

Betty Sue thanked him when he took his position in the driver's seat.

The restaurant wasn't far, and before they knew it they were seated in an outdoor patio overlooking a large pond. The music was upbeat but low, and the energy comfortable and relaxing. They both ordered a glass of wine and munched on appetizers while they waited for their dinner. Betty Sue was visiting from Florida, where she'd moved after her husband died, she told Dwight. She missed him. She missed home, but she was having a hard time emotionally moving on where she was.

Dwight was bewildered at so many of their similarities and synchronicities in their lives, like both of them attending Catholic school, both of their spouses passing from cancer, and even having the same favorite dessert (bread pudding). Conversation was easy, without expectation or judgment, and before they knew it the restaurant was lighting the propane heaters and turning on the outside patio lights.

"We should get back to see how Beth made out with Kat," Betty Sue softly suggested.

Dwight agreed and tried to call the waiter over for the bill.

"Beth paid for this ahead of time," Betty Sue reminded Dwight.

Dwight, being old-fashioned, made sure to leave an extra tip on the table. Then he helped Betty Sue back into the car, making their way back to the clinic.

"I'd like to do this again," Dwight said. "Of course, I'd pay."

Betty Sue blushed in the dusk. It'd been years since she had been asked out on a date, and although she did love Florida, it was typically the ninety-year-old men in the grocery store who were trying to pick her up in the produce section, and probably hoping she'd cook for them.

"I leave next week, but I'm sure we can find a time to do something."

Dwight smiled and realized it was probably his first smile in close to a year.

When they got back to the clinic, Beth was just shutting the lights off. Kat was sound asleep on a blanket in the back room and didn't even lift her head. Dwight gently ran his hand over her head and petted her ears before giving her a kiss on the forehead. "See you tomorrow, old girl. Sleep well."

"She's doing great, Dwight. Let that medicine do its job. I think she'll need a week plus of some oral antibiotics, but otherwise I think you'll see her chipper self real soon."

Dwight choked a thank you, swallowing his tears.

"I'll see you tomorrow afternoon," she said, walking Dwight and her mom outside and locking the door behind her.

Dwight said his good-byes and went home to a quiet house.

That night he tossed and turned, swearing that he could hear Kat whining and then remembering that she was at the clinic. He woke after having a dream that Sharon and Kat were standing side by side, smiling at him. Sharon told him in the dream that she would take care of Kat until he got there. The sheets were soaked with sweat and he decided to just get up and make some coffee because sound sleep obviously wasn't going to happen. He looked at the clock and it was only 4 a.m. The older he got, the earlier he got up. He used to joke with his parents to stop going to bed right after supper and maybe they could sleep in, but now he'd become them, and no matter what time he went to sleep he seemed to get up earlier than the birds. He was startled out of his thoughts by his cell phone ringing and when he saw who it was, he knew.

Kat had passed sometime during the night, Dr. Seagram informed him. She'd gone to check on her around 3 a.m., but she must've passed soon after they all left that night. She wasn't certain the exact reason, but she thought perhaps Kat had either liver or bladder cancer, and she asked if he wanted an autopsy. Stunned by the news, he simply hung up the phone, grabbed his coat, and got into his car, driving to the clinic.

Betty Sue opened the door for him and gave him a friendly hug, walking him back to where Kat was curled up on the blanket, looking as if she was peacefully sleeping.

"You're sure …?" Dwight began.

Dr. Seagram gravely nodded her head, wiping away her tears. She'd always wanted to be an animal healer, not just a doctor, and death never stopped having an impact on her. She was human and an animal lover, and hoped to never be bitter and hard that she couldn't react.

Betty Sue handed Dwight and Beth both a cup of coffee and placed two folding chairs down in front of them.

"Grief turns our world upside down," Betty Sue softly muttered to nobody in general. "We take a risk every time we love someone, but I believe that the risk of love outweighs the pain of loss, we just don't see it in the midst of the loss."

"Would you like her cremated, Dwight?" Dr. Seagram asked.

Dwight set his untouched cup of coffee down and nodded. He walked over to Kat and sat beside her one last time, putting his head into her neck and nuzzled her. "I know you found Mom, Kat. Run free. I'm so sorry for not being here with you."

Beth hung her head, feeling guilty for giving him false hope and not allowing him those last moments. It was her fault, she argued in her head. It was all her fault.

Dwight stood up and, without looking at anyone or calling out a good-bye, he left.

Dr. Seagram and Betty Sue both tried calling Dwight several times that day, only to get no answer.

"You did nothing wrong," Betty Sue told her daughter. "You had hope. It was just Kat's time."

Beth was a friend of mine for many years, but I hadn't heard from her for years, so I was surprised when she called me and asked if we could meet to talk. Between her busy schedule and my own busy schedule somehow we both had an opening the next day, and she met me at my office with Starbucks in hand and a big hug.

"I've never had a problem before, Kristy," she said, pursing her lips.

"I know you, Beth. I know the big heart you have, which is why you went to school for what you did and why you do what you do."

It was true. Beth worked hard and never asked for a cent from her parents for school. She wanted to change the world and traveled all over learning about animal science, biology, and zoology. She gave up a semester of school to volunteer abroad at various rescues, and she was one of the best in her field, but I also knew she wasn't numb to death. It just wasn't her way. She was the type who would hide, but once everyone was gone would have her breakdown. She felt everything, but sitting across from me it was like she was trying to convince me that she didn't, or shouldn't, or hadn't. I knew that wasn't true.

"I really thought I could've saved Kat, though, Kristy. Maybe I'm getting arrogant and thinking I'm an animal God. I missed something this time, and I don't miss anything."

I raised my eyebrow at her.

"See? I *am* arrogant!" Beth croaked.

I laughed in response because that wasn't true at all, and I told her so.

"It's not arrogant to be educated and skilled, but I think maybe you've forgotten that even science has variables."

"Like when it's their time to go, it's their time to go," Beth pondered.

"Something like that. You can't save everyone, but you do a real good job. I'm not always a fan of the saying *everything happens for a reason*, but I have a feeling that this is the case here."

"So now what?" Beth asked.

"I have a suspicion that your dad, Dwight's wife, and even Kat are on to something bigger than we know right now. In fact, I can guarantee it," I smiled.

Even after our talk, Beth still couldn't help but feel like she missed something, and she dug her heals into her work so she wouldn't think about it. It was a week after Kat's passing when the ashes came. Betty Sue postponed her trip back to Florida because she was worried about her daughter and she was worried about Dwight. Without any answer still, Betty Sue decided to take Kat's box and deliver it herself.

It was before eight in the morning when she stood on the porch stoop with the wooden box in her arms. Dwight's car was parked in the driveway, but several newspapers were scattered about behind it, and his mailbox was stuffed so full that it was mostly open. *Maybe I should call the police for a well check*, she thought for a moment, but instead she knocked. "C'mon, Kat, help me get you to your dad," she whispered. She heard rustling around in the house, so she knocked louder. "I'm not going away, Dwight, so just open the door."

A moment later, Dwight opened the door, looking disheveled and smelling sour, obviously not showering for days. Unapologetically he opened his door to Betty Sue and walked back in without seeing if she was following. She was.

"I know it's hard. I know more than you know I know," Betty Sue lectured. "But Sharon or Kat wouldn't want you like this and you know it."

Dwight sat in his chair, numb.

"These are Kat's remains. Her paw print is on top of the box, just as much as it is engraved on your heart. I made sure to get that before they took her." Betty Sue pushed the box in his arms and looked to see if she got any reaction from him, but there was none.

"I wasn't so sure I'd get through losing Libby last year. She'd been there through all the ups and downs of losing my husband and when my son refused to talk to me. Then I decided to move, and Libby died the night before in her sleep. All I could think was I was being punished for something, you know?"

Dwight hadn't moved or reacted one bit, but Betty Sue continued, "Then I thought how much Libby would hate for me to be so sad. So I started to write down all the things that Libby did that made me happy or laugh. You're probably not a poem guy, but I found this poem and I read it over and over again. It's called "I'm Still Here" and it explains how we might not see them, but they are here with us, by our sides, only their pain is gone. It's our pain that is unbearable."

Dwight hugged Kat's box, tears falling.

"Thank you," he said somberly.

"Now, let's go to breakfast," Betty Sue said. "Well, after you shower. I'll clean up here in the meantime."

Dwight had never met such a strong woman before, besides his Sharon. He was in awe of her perseverance and will, and he couldn't help but obey her orders. "I think I'm going to call you Colonel," he joked, walking to the bathroom after grabbing a towel and some clean clothes from the laundry room.

"I'm okay with that," Betty Sue laughed, and she started to load the dishwasher. She took out her cell phone after the last dish was in and called the clinic. Beth sounded out of breath and distracted.

"Mom, I can't talk. I have a litter of puppies that I found by my back dumpster. They can't be more than a few weeks old, and I have to figure out what I'm going to do with them. Can we talk later?"

Betty Sue hung up the phone, gently knocked on the bathroom door, and told Dwight to kick it into gear. They had an emergency to attend to.

Confused, Dwight slid on his jeans and a T-shirt and put on his shoes. With his hair still wet, he raced out the door and sat in the passenger seat of Betty Sue's car. Running through McDonald's, they ordered some coffee and hot cakes, before driving to the clinic.

"Betty Sue, what are we ...?"

But Betty Sue ignored him and grabbed the takeout bags, leaving Dwight to carry the cups of coffee. He followed her into the clinic, where Beth sat on the floor surrounded by six black and white furry puppies. Betty Sue and Dwight went into action, taking bottles and helping to feed the pups until they all plopped down on the floor in food comas. Dwight couldn't help but notice that they were in the same spot that Kat took her last breath without him, and yet now so much life danced around without even a blink.

"How dare those people," Dwight growled. "How could any-one leave innocent puppies to fend for themselves?"

"It happens often," Beth said. "Two years ago, a car screeched up to the clinic and threw a cat inside the door right at me. He'd been burned and had a broken jaw. That's him over there, lying on the counter. I named him Brando because he rules this place like the Godfather."

The group laughed.

"He had to have three major surgeries, but he seems to have adapted."

As if on cue, Brando looked over at the three humans and loudly let out a meow.

"Then last year I had a litter of pit bulls who'd been shot at. Four of the five survived. I thankfully found them all homes. I could go on and on, but it's depressing. Now I have to figure out what to do with these guys and gals. At least they all had each other."

The puppies were all curled up on top of one another, and Dwight thought how right Dr. Seagram was. Maybe trying to do everything alone all of the time wasn't proactive. Maybe you did need others to help survive. A puppy got up and fell back down, falling right back to sleep.

Two weeks later, Dwight took two of the puppy's home with him, naming them Tom and Jerry. Betty Sue had gone back to Flor-ida, but they talked several times a day on the phone, laughing at the silly puppy escapades.

"I wonder if Kat is jealous," Dwight said to Betty Sue one after-noon as they chatted on the phone.

"Are you worried about Kat or about Sharon?"

"Touché," Dwight laughed.

It wasn't more than six months after that Betty Sue and Dwight were married.

"I'm not getting any younger," Betty Sue squawked. "Anyway, I was tired of being around all the older geezers in Florida, and Beth needed my help," she explained to her friends.

Dwight had never smiled or laughed as much as he did with Betty Sue, or at Betty Sue. Her outspoken honesty was refreshing. He loved Sharon, and always would, nothing would ever take that piece of love away from him. Just as he loved Tom and Jerry but would never stop loving Kat. He realized there was enough love in him for everyone.

After Betty Sue and Dwight said their vows, they had a small dinner with friends and family. He pulled Beth aside right before dessert. "Through the heartache of losing Kat, I gained a wife, a daughter, and a menagerie of animals. I've grieved and moved forward, Beth, I don't want you to feel bad anymore, okay?"

Beth wiped her eyes and nodded.

"Plus, I get free vet care, right?"

Beth playfully swatted his shoulder and walked him back to her mom.

It's a common worry that your pet feels replaced, but the reality is nobody, our pet or our people, can ever be replaced. Instead, you simply add more love to your heart. Our pets and our people on the Other Side are able to see, hear, and feel what you are going through and the last thing they want to do is deny you joy.

CHAMP

Grady laid her head on the tiled white bathroom floor. She couldn't feel the hardness of the ground or the coldness of the tiles, all she felt was her heart aching. No, not just aching, splintered and elec-trified. With each thought, each physical movement, and every emotion, Grady felt something shattering within, and what scared her was that she didn't even care.

"Get off the floor, Grady," her husband begged.

The sobs erupted again and her so-called waterproof mascara dripped black gobs on the recently bleached floor. "I'm fine right where I'm at," she muttered through her tears.

"No, you aren't fine on the floor. I'm not fine with you on the floor," Jessie said, this time sounding more agitated than sympa-thetic. Sighing, he sat down next to his wife, his back resting against the wooden vanity, and gently pulled her to him.

"But ... you ... don't ... understand!" She wept and placed her head in his lap as he stroked her shoulder length brown hair.

"Tell me what I don't understand, Grady?"

"You don't understand how it feels to have lost that contract at work, the one that I worked on for two years. A company that I worked with and dedicated myself to, and then to be told that I was no longer a good fit. You don't understand how it feels when your mom gives you that disappointed look, even after thirty-something years and all I've ever wanted was her approval. You don't under-stand how it feels to lose a baby that I carried and loved for ten weeks, and will love forever, but will never be able to hold. You don't understand how it feels to be a complete failure!"

"The job, Grady—there will be others. Too bad for them. Your mom—again, too bad for her that she doesn't realize what a fabu-lous daughter she has. And the baby ... I'm mourning too. Proba-bly not quite like you. But none of this equates to failure. You are the strongest, most incredible person that I know, and you've over-come every step of the way, and you will do the same this time."

Jessie's eyes began to mist. What Grady didn't understand is that he felt like a failure for not being able to help her not feel like a failure. "There's a line in an old hymn that says, 'Let there be peace in the world and let it begin with me.' I can't give you peace, only you can give you peace, Grady, but I'm by your side through it all."

I saw Grady for an appointment soon after her miscarriage and I was excited that her guides showed me another baby on the way, and soon. Not a replacement for the baby she lost, but it was nice to give good news. Although Grady felt like a failure at that moment in time, she realized that most everything she festered over couldn't be controlled.

But it wasn't just a baby that I saw; I also saw a golden retriever that stood proudly next to an older lady who was holding the baby in her arms.

"You need to talk about Champ," the spirit urged.

"Grady, there is a lady who is holding your baby, but who also has a beautiful fur baby she said was named Champ."

Grady sucked in her breath and looked at me wide eyed. "Champ?" she asked, swallowing hard.

"He looks like a golden retriever?" I said in question.

Grady nodded. Avoiding any eye contact, she played with a strand of yarn on her sweater for a minute before speaking again. "Does Grandma forgive me?"

I looked at Grady and then again to the lady on the Other Side, who looked agitated that Grady couldn't hear her speak or feel her touch. "There's nothing to forgive. Tell her that. She needs to let this go. She didn't kill Champ. Cancer killed Champ."

I shared the message with Grady, who didn't seem to believe me.

"Grady, if anyone was mad at you, why would your grandma come through, holding your baby, and standing next to a dog you think you killed? Champ wouldn't show up for the session if he thought you did anything negligent to him."

Psychically cancer looks like chicken pox to me, only dark and murky colored. Although we are healthy on the Other Side, for validation purposes those on the Other Side will show me what caused their passing. Champ looked as if cancer had spread throughout his whole body, beginning in his abdomen area.

"You most certainly didn't give him cancer," I tried to impress on her.

"No, I didn't give him cancer. But I promised to take care of him, and I didn't," Grady sighed. "Maybe that's why I lost the baby. Some karmic punishment."

I stared at her in disbelief and thought for a moment before I said anything. It was obvious this was a weight she'd held on to for quite some time.

"Grady, your grandma would never punish you like that. God wouldn't punish you like that. And Champ would never want you to feel that way. Karma doesn't work like how many believe. What you are doing to yourself right here, right now, that is karma. You are taking your grief and turning it into something that isn't yours to carry."

Grady's grandma, Stella, had gone into the hospital for massive abdominal pain, only to find out that she had a tumor in her colon, and it was cancerous. The surgery and recovery would take weeks, so Grady did the only thing she could do, she took Champ home with her.

He pouted and was sad, not understanding the change or where his beloved mom was. When Stella was released to the rehabilitation clinic, Grady snuck Champ in to see her. Some say that animals don't smile or laugh, but then those would probably be people who've never had a beloved furry friend. Champ was so excited, but even as a puppy was gentle and sweet, and as if understanding that he had to be quiet or else he'd be booted out of the facility, he showed his happiness by laying his head against Stella's scarred tummy, letting her stroke his head and ears. The time spent there felt like just minutes when it really was over an hour, but Stella and Grady knew they'd worn out their welcome.

"I'll try and sneak him over next week," Grady promised, giving a kiss good-bye on the cheek of her grandma and grabbing her grandma's load of laundry.

"Okay, hon. I'll call you after dinner to see how your job interview went. To the moon and back."

"To the moon and back," Grady repeated. It was their good-bye since Grady first learned to speak. Stella used to tell Grady that she fell in love with her the moment her mom said she was pregnant. Grady used to tease that that wasn't anything. Grady loved her for her entire life—almost twenty-four years.

Their relationship was so much different than the relationship she had with her parents. Stella never criticized or looked disapproving at her, even when she made stupid mistakes and had crazy ideas. Stella helped Grady color outside the lines, giving her the extra push to finish college and even told her to date, don't settle. "You have to test drive a bunch of cars before you know which one you like. The outside might look pretty, but that doesn't mean it's stable and reliable," Stella would say. Grady wondered if her mom was jealous of her relationship with Stella, but no matter, she was grateful that she had her.

Champ remained glued to Stella and, although always well-behaved, Grady had to gently pull on his collar to get him to leave. He put his head down and moaned.

"Next week, bud. We'll see her next week, okay?" Grady promised.

Grady took Champ back to her home and got ready for the job interview. It was her first real job interview, and she was nervous and a bit frazzled. Since coming home from the rehab center Champ had laid on the couch and slept. He didn't want his favorite yellow tennis ball or his snack, and he didn't even budge when she scratched his ear. *Maybe it wasn't a good idea to take him to visit,* she thought. *He's probably depressed all over again.*

Grady's cell phone rang as she was rushing out the door, but she ignored it. She had to be in the right mind-set. This opportunity could be something big, she just knew it.

Walking out of the interview with a huge smile, and hiring paperwork in hand, she unlocked her car and slid in. Grabbing her phone from her purse, she was surprised to see several voice messages. The first one from Stella's rehabilitation center, another from her mom, and another from her dad. "Uh oh," she said to herself, "I bet we were found out and in trouble."

But that wasn't it at all. Stella had gone into cardiac arrest soon after her visit with Grady and Champ and had passed away.

The days leading up to the funeral were a blur of phone calls, preparations, and plain numbness. Champ was still acting out of sorts and it made Grady wonder if he'd known something.

"Maybe I should bring him to the funeral home," Grady suggested to her parents, who told her that was a ridiculous idea. Before leaving for the funeral, she bent down to give Grady a hug and a kiss, not concerned with yellow fur on her black dress that she was certain her mom would nitpick. "You're all I have left of Grandma now, Champ. We'll get through this together. We have to."

The day was a long one filled with forced smiles and relatives she'd never seen before. If she heard one more time how her grandma was in a better place, or she must be so happy being with Ed, her grandpa, or how she isn't in pain any longer, she was going to scream. How on earth did anyone think that made the hurt any better?

Kicking off her shoes at home, Grady grabbed the mail and called for Champ. "I'll get the ice cream and you get your bone and let's cuddle and watch *Sleepless in Seattle*, Champ."

But Champ didn't come running to her, not even when she filled his dog dish with food. He wasn't on the couch, and he wasn't in his dog bed either. She found him in her laundry room lying on Stella's robe, the one she brought back with her to wash. It looked like he was sleeping, so she bent down to nudge him only to realize he had died. She wasn't sure what the sound that came out of her mouth was or who she called or who came over and took him to the veterinarian. Or how she ended up in her bed with blankets up to her chin.

The veterinarian did an autopsy upon Grady's request, only to find that Champ had stomach cancer that had spread, unbeknownst to anyone.

"They say that animals can absorb our energy, our emotion, and even our physical ailments," I told Grady, both of us tearing up as she talked about the experience.

"Do you think he knew that Grandma was going to die that day?"

I nodded. "They are quite perceptive, which is why there are some animals who can detect cancer, diabetes, and other ailments. It's a sixth sense that we all have, we are just bombarded by real life problems that weigh us down. Our pets don't have to worry about how the car is being paid or how the snow is going to be shoveled. They can stay in the now, not worrying about the past or the future."

"So nobody is mad at me?"

"I promise I would tell you if that were the case, but it isn't. Oh, and by the way, Grandma is showing a new baby and a new puppy too. Apparently, she thinks you're Wonder Woman!"

Grady laughed. "Yes to the baby; no to the puppy. Tell Grandma one thing at a time."

"Honestly, I think Champ is gifting you a puppy from the Other Side," I shared.

"A stuffed animal kind, right?"

"Maybe. Doubtful. But maybe."

I ended the session by giving her some soul work to do in order to start the healing and to stop the self-blame game. You can try it too.

Soul Work

Share your story—Share your reactions, your feelings of failure, your feelings of success, and everything in between. Even if it doesn't make sense and even if it revolves around things that are not under your control, it helps to begin the grief process. It might be through journaling or saying it aloud to a friend or family member, but express it in some manner instead of leaving it bottled up inside.

Get help—It could be professional counseling, a church, your community, a hypnotherapist, your family doctor, etc., but by seeking help and receiving resources, you won't feel quite so alone.

Self-care—Take care of yourself through exercise, nutrition, and relaxation techniques (yoga, meditation, Pilates, etc.).

Color therapy—Put away the black and brown clothes and pull out something bright to wear, even if you feel less than merry and bright.

Surround yourself with love—Surround yourself with family, friends, and pets that you love.

It begins with you—Nobody controls you or your reactions. Happiness begins with you. Peace begins with you. Healing begins with you.

Grady and her husband Jessie sent me a card with a beautiful picture of her holding a healthy baby boy, born December 23. They named him Callum, an Irish name meaning calm and peace. She also decided to open her own consulting company where she can use all of her gifts, a dream she's had since she was a little girl and shared with Stella. And her mom—well, Grady now realizes that, although it still hurts, she can only control her reaction. She said she visualizes a blue healing light emitting from her own heart to her mom every time she criticizes, hoping that one day her mom will realize that the healing begins with her too.

> *Jessie and I were on our way to pick up some things for Callum before I had him and in front of the shop was a lady with a litter of puppies,"* Grady wrote. *"He's not a goldie, he's just a mixed breed, but this is Champ the second. I guess I am Wonder Woman.*

You are brave, but you are human. You are allowed to hurt. You are allowed to be afraid, and you are even allowed to whine and have self-pity. You are human. Yes, you are brave, but you have to be good to yourself and stop apologizing for being human. A dog doesn't apologize for being a dog, or a cat for being a cat.

We put so much pressure on ourselves and that goes for putting a lot of pressure on others to do and say exactly what we think they should. It's just never good enough. It can always be better, and yet with that mentality there is no healing for you or others, it is just noise.

Cats take time to bath and nap in the sunshine. Dogs take time to play. Self-care isn't a luxury—it is fuel for your soul.

KIT CAT

A friend of mine was having some interesting paranormal experiences and asked me if a past-life regression might hold the key to some questions. I didn't think it would hurt, so she set up an appointment with another friend of mine, Gayle, a gifted, skilled, and certified hypnotherapist that was across the hall from my office at the time.

Kit was a bit nervous, so with Gayle's permission I came in with her.

Hypnotherapy is like a guided meditation. The hypnotherapist uses positive suggestion to bring about subconscious change to thoughts, feelings, and behavior. It is a relaxation technique that is helpful in everything from pain control to stress. Always in control, and not like the stage shows that you see where the hypnotist makes them cluck like a chicken, it's a very helpful and healing technique. Everything that we experience, good and bad, is stored in the files of our subconscious. Past-life regression uses the same technique, only you are going further back in the files to recover memories and experiences.

I'd had plenty of hypnotherapy sessions with Gayle, most of which I fell asleep during, which has no bearing on the healing. But, it is always my best sleep. So I figured I'd lay in the recliner next to Kit and, if anything, rest.

As Gayle began her hypnosis, I began to fall under too, only I become a spectator in Kit's past-life experience.

Her first experience was somber and detailed with personal situations that helped unlock the doors to her personal worries and concerns. Once she completed that journey, Gayle asked that she go deeper and to explain out loud what she saw.

"I'm running," Kit said in a far-off tone.

"Where are you running?" Gayle probed.

"I'm barefoot and the ground is dirt and hard. I have to run," Kit said in a monotone voice.

"What are you running from?"

As Gayle asked questions, there I was in Kit's subconscious experience, trying to reach Kit unsuccessfully and trying to telepathically reach Gayle to tell her to stop, to call off the regression and wake her. Instead I felt stuck, forced to witness.

"Oh my God," Kit screamed

"What's going on, Kit?" Gayle calmly asked.

"There's a mountain lion. It's going to eat me!" she exclaimed, fidgeting in the leather recliner, but not waking.

Just then my eyes snapped open and I saw the large cat leap over Gayle and promptly disappear.

Gayle looked at me, surprised. Realizing that this was not a healthy experience, she quickly brought her back awake.

Kit rubbed her eyes and sat up. "No wonder I hate cats!" she laughed. "This explains everything!"

Kit came into this lifetime allergic to cats and just plain hating them. That was until the regression. Although her allergies didn't disappear, the suppressed fear and hatred of cats healed. For a quick minute, she thought of adopting a cat.

The odd thing was that part of her paranormal experiences included scratches on the walls, floors, and even on her and her other family members—that was until the regression when that all disappeared.

Just as a human can't be replaced, neither can your pet. For some, the best way to grieve is to adopt another pet immediately, but this isn't a one size fits all world, especially when it comes to grief. Just know that you will know the right time. You aren't dishonoring your pet on the Other Side by loving another. There will always be a loving pet waiting for your love, and your pet on the Other Side will embrace your new pet into their family just as you do.

~ 10 ~

GIFTS FROM THE OTHER SIDE

Pet spirits don't go to one place on the Other Side and human spirits to another. They are connected to one another because they are connected to you.

ANNIE

Nathan was always traveling. It was simply part of his job, and his wife knew that before they even married. It didn't mean that she liked it, though. It wasn't that Andrea didn't trust Nathan, it was that she always had this sinking feeling in her stomach each time he left for a long trip.

"You're being silly," Nathan would tell her, always with a kiss on the forehead and another on the lips. "You know that I always come back. This isn't good-bye!"

As much as Nathan tried to reassure Andy, she couldn't shake the anxiety, so much that she went to her doctor for medication. Although it took the edge off, she still felt uneasy.

It was June 2015 when her intuition turned into reality, and the phone call came that her husband had been traveling on the freeway to his account when a truck tire blew and flew over the freeway's median and into oncoming traffic. Nathan tried to avoid the debris, but there was nothing he could do about the tractor trailer on one side and the wall on the other. First responders called him dead on arrival.

The funeral was surreal as Andy sat with their four teenagers in the front row of the church. It was the church they tried to attend every Sunday and holiday, the church they were married at, and the church where their children were baptized and confirmed. Nathan's family and friends were simply numb to the fact that he wouldn't be walking in the door with his crooked smile and infectious laughter.

Andrea had made an appointment with me, specifically to speak to her mom, never imagining that her appointment would fall on the day after Nathan's funeral. I tell clients to wait close to a year after the passing. Not only for an adjustment period for those here but also because it's an adjustment period for those on the Other Side. They need to find their voice, so to speak. When Andrea sat down, she was surrounded by loved ones, and front and center was a handsome man who showed me his wedding ring, a sign for me that he was her spouse.

"There's a man here who says he loves you very much, and that you were right, he should've listened. He's sorry."

Andrea began to cry.

"Although he wishes he were here, he wants you to know that it isn't good-bye."

Andrea looked up at me and asked me to repeat myself.

"He says this isn't good-bye, it's a different kind of hello."

It was what he said after every conversation on the phone and every time he walked out the door on his travels, Andrea confirmed. Even in the afterlife he was letting her know he would be around.

The session was over and I walked Andrea to the door, but I felt Nathan's energy nudge me, so I turned around to see him standing there with a surprise. "He also has a large gray bird with him," I added.

Andrea gasped. "A bird?" she asked. "Like a parrot?"

"Nathan said he wanted you to know he found him."

Andrea touched her hand to her heart. "That's Benny," she smiled. "He was an African gray parrot and I had him for twenty-one years. One day, I woke up and he had passed. Ironically, that night I had a blind date and I wanted to cancel because I was so upset."

"And that blind date wouldn't have been Nathan, would it?" I leaned forward with interest.

"It was Nathan," she confirmed. "I always wanted another bird, and Nathan would tell me to just get one, but Benny was special. Then I had kids, and I just didn't have enough time to spend with a pet."

Birds can be amazing companions, but they do take a lot of time, energy, and patience. Although I've never had a bird as a pet, a friend of mine has a couple parrots and she says it's like having a toddler for decades.

"Nathan found Benny. Or Benny found Nathan. That's nice," Andrea giggled and gave me a hug as she left.

It was a few months after our session when I received a panicked voice mail asking me to call Andrea immediately. Immediately for me can't always be immediately, but once my office sessions were complete, I dialed her number and waited for her to pick up. Without even a greeting, Andrea breathlessly started bab-bling about a bird and Nathan and not sure what to do and she thought it was a ghost. I tried to connect the dots, but I was a bit confused and had to ask her to slow down a bit and start over.

"I came home from taking the girls to school and sitting on the deck was a bird," she started after taking some calming breaths.

"That's nice." I wondered why a bird on the deck, outside, was so unusual.

"Kristy, it looks just like Benny, my African gray."

Then it made sense why she was freaked out. She continued telling me that she brought the bird inside and called the local ani-mal shelter in case someone was missing him.

"He talks too."

"That's amazing!"

"No, its plain spooky, Kristy. He says Annie," she exclaimed from the other end of the phone. "That's what Nathan called me."

"It's probably his owner's name," I reasoned with her, although I knew that the spiritual world wasn't always so cut and dry.

"Do you think it's Nathan? Or Benny? Or both? Can they rein-carnate like that?" Andrea fretted. "How can I keep Nathan in a cage? Oh my God, Kristy, what am I going to tell the kids?"

I couldn't help but laugh out loud at her panic and an image of her explaining to her kids that their dad had come back to life in the form of a bird.

When my mom passed away, I was given the opportunity to rescue a Siamese and tabby mixed kitten with beautiful white fur, a smudging of gray, and bright blue eyes. My husband sucked his breath in when he saw her.

"It's your mother," he told me. "It's her hair color. It's her eye color. It's her."

"It's not my mother," I reassured him, snuggling the kitten in my arms. "She's just sent from my mother."

There are many theories about reincarnation, especially with regards to animals to human, and human to animals. Your Uncle Sid did not come back as the flea on your dog, although you may think that was like his personality. Our loved ones on the Other Side want us to be happy, and so they often will send us pets to bring more joy into our life. They can channel through the animal, but they aren't the animal or become the animal. They may have traits of your past pet or past human, and this is because they were chosen from your loved ones on the Other Side.

Andrea calmed down a bit after I explained that if she put the bird in the cage, she wasn't caging her past husband. After waiting a week without any word from the shelters, she received a phone call letting her know that the bird did in fact have an owner, but they didn't want it anymore and she could keep it if she wanted.

"How could you keep a pet for years and years only to throw them away? I just don't understand," she grunted in disgust.

"Their trash is your treasure, though, right? And nothing in life is coincidence. Although it's sad, it was also an amazing sign too."

It ended up that the bird's name was Annie, and Andrea kept her. Last year, Annie passed away and although Andrea grieved, she was grateful for the time she was able to spend with her, giving her a happy home. She also knew that Nathan and Benny welcomed her into their family on the Other Side, just like she and her kids did for the short time they had her.

When taking on the responsibility of a pet, it should be for forever. A pet should be loved and treated like a member of the family. Not left alone in the backyard, chained up in the yard, replaced by a younger pet, or dropped off on the side of the road. They should not be neglected or abused. They offer you unconditional love and joy and if you can't do the same, there is someone else who can and will.

BE MERRY

Faye sat looking at the twinkling of the Christmas lights, wishing she felt some holiday cheer, but all of her own merry left when she received word a couple months before that her husband, a Green Beret, died overseas in what the Army was referring to as an accident. After several tours, all to the Middle East, her family was used to Derek's absences, but they never imagined he'd never return home.

The quiet of the early morning was interrupted by an odd sound at the front porch.

"Come in," she yelled out, figuring it was Derek's family or hers, coming to make sure she actually got out of bed. It was easier to stay hidden under the covers, pretending and wishing it wasn't real. But the noise continued, so, reluctantly, Faye got up to look out the door only to see a small white kitten pressed against the screen door, shivering. Faye opened the door, bent down, and picked up the furry bundle. She looked around, but nobody else was there. The kitten nuzzled herself into Faye's neck with a purr just as the rest of the family ran down the steps to begin the Christmas morning festivities.

"A kitten!" Dakota, Faye's five-year-old son exclaimed. "Santa brought a kitten?!"

"I think it's lost, Dakota. We need to find its owner."

But Dakota wasn't listening. He gently took the kitten from his mom. "I bet Dad sent her for us. We should call her Derek!" Dakota danced around the room, ignoring the gifts underneath the Christmas tree.

"We're not calling her Derek, stupid," Rachael said, petting the small kitten behind its ears. "There will never be another Dad, plus it's a girl," Rachael, who was twelve years old, said.

"We can't name her anything. She's not ours," Faye scolded.

"I think she is, Mom. I think Daddy sent her. We should call her Merry. Dad wanted us to be happy, and this is a reminder."

"Hi, Merry," Dakota whispered, stroking the kitten.

Faye rolled her eyes, but the kitten certainly took to the household at once, as if it belonged. She curled up on the couch for a nap while the kids ran to the Christmas tree to open their gifts.

After the presents were opened, Faye looked through the lost animal ads on her computer, but nothing matched the tiny white kitten with blue-gray eyes. Hesitating at placing her own found ad, wondering if it was a sign from her husband, she quickly discounted it and wrote:

Found white kitten with gray ears on doorstep. About six weeks old. No collar. Contact me if yours, adding her cross streets.

But there were no calls or e-mails, only friends on Facebook noting that it had to be a gift from Heaven. Again, skeptical, the next morning Faye took it to her veterinarian. As if she had any time for this, she balked. Family was flying in for the funeral and her house was a mess from the holiday, but still she sat in the waiting room with the tiny kitten sitting content in her lap.

"There's no chip," the veterinarian confirmed after scanning its back. "And she's not neutered, actually too young to be yet. Can I tell you something, Faye?"

Faye looked up with question.

"I know it sounds odd and all, but do you think this is Derek's way of saying he's okay?"

Faye laughed. It was what everyone was saying, but to hear a professional say it seemed even stranger, yet hard to not ignore.

"If someone comes in with a flyer, I'll let you know, but honestly I don't think that'll happen. I think this is your gift from Heaven."

Faye thought for a moment before asking. She felt silly, but it was something weighing on her mind. "Doctor? Do you believe that humans reincarnate into animals? I mean, do you think this is Derek?" Faye whispered, feeling even more ridiculous once the words were out.

The doctor thought for a moment before beginning, "Let me first say that I was raised Catholic, so the thought of reincarnation wasn't something spoke of or accepted in our house." The doctor laughed. "It was something my mom said Shirley McClain created."

Faye and the doctor both laughed before he began again, "But, I have seen miracles, and I've seen unexplained oddities that I can't wrap my brain around. It's made me realize that I don't know everything, and I probably won't until I'm over there on the Other Side and I can ask the big guy myself. Boy, I have some questions. I don't believe that humans come back as animals, though. I believe human souls send animals to us. In some Native American myths, it is believed the soul of a loved one can send an animal form to send love and messages. Some souls send butterflies, birds, or squirrels. You got a kitten. I believe that our loved ones, including our past animals, can affect or influence here. They may even show similar personalities or attitudes. Or maybe even what they call channel through."

The doctor looked a bit out of place and then asked if he could share something with Faye, who nodded curiously.

"It was about a month after my mom passed away when a patient came in with a kitten he couldn't keep, and he asked if I could find it a home. This kitten had the bluest of blue eyes, just like my mom did, and for a brief moment I thought maybe. My mom was incredibly shy and aloof, and so was this kitten. I ended up taking in the kitten as my own. My wife told me to name it after my mom. I thought that was horrendous and if my mom could haunt me, she would for that. So I didn't. I don't believe it was my mom, but I believe I was gifted Toby from my mom. I think Merry is your gift from Derek, Faye. I really do."

Faye thanked the doctor for his candid confession and advice. Swooping Merry into her arms, she went back home and deleted her found ad. How many times was she going to be told that the kitten was a gift from Heaven before she believed it herself?

Faye had an appointment with me right before the first anniversary of Derek's passing. Derek showed up in spirit and told me to ask Faye how the kitten was. Faye just laughed in response. She didn't need the validation, but it was nice to hear it again.

"He also wants you to ask Rachael about the note because it may clear things up a bit."

Faye shook her head in confusion, but she promised she'd ask her after school.

"He plays with the kitten too," I told her. "And the electricity."

As if on cue, Faye's phone decided to shut off and on again, making us laugh.

Faye didn't want to tell Rachael she saw a medium, so without mentioning me she asked Faye if she knew anything about a note and her dad. Rachael blushed.

"I left a note for Daddy in the casket, and I asked him to send me a kitten. I know it was stupid, and I didn't really think he'd do it. How'd you know?"

Faye avoided the question; she simply laughed and asked her what else she asked him for.

Rachael returned with a giggle and hugged her mom. "I asked him to make you happy again."

The holidays can be extra tough. Include your loved ones on the Other Side, pets and people alike, in your Christmas festivities. In a quiet, comfortable place, sit near a picture of them. Have a conversation with them, telling them about your days, and saying everything you need or desire to say. Listen—remember the sound of their voice, how they spoke, the way they made you feel when you were near them. Holidays, anniversaries, birthdays, and special celebrations have a way of opening up the scars that you thought had healed, but our loved ones want us to not live in the past, but remember it. They also want us to include them in our present. That in itself is the best gift we can give ourselves, and them too.

Conclusion

How lucky I am to have something
that makes saying good-bye so hard.
—Winnie the Pooh

It was through my own grief of my beloved Australian shepherd Guinness that I began to research and write this book. As I further connected to my grief, I began to find myself vibrationally aligned to others with membership in the Heartbreak Club. When we welcome a pet into our life, we know there will one day be a good-bye, but that doesn't make it any less sad. They become more than an animal, they become family. They help set our routines, they depend on us for their needs, and they offer us unconditional love. So whether you've lost your family member unexpectedly or you were able to spend many years with your pet and prepared for the ending, mourning and grieving isn't crazy, it's normal, it feels unbearable, and there may be moments in the day you wonder how to cope.

Your heart will be broken, but just think of how much love you were given in the time you were given. You will miss them. You will look for them and then remember. You will talk to friends and family members who don't understand your sadness. And you will talk to friends and family members who completely understand. Not only will their memory be ingrained within your heart and soul, your love remains with them for their eternity. You will see them again when you make your transition to the Other Side, but you can see, hear, sense, and even communicate with them from the Other Side. So often they want you to know that they made their trip and that they are okay. They want to offer their forgiveness if you need it. They want to send their love to you when you are sad. They also want you to heal and not think you failed as a parent.

Animals have a magical way about them; after all they are spiritual beings. They can comfort the sick and heartbroken, they remain steadfast to even the disloyal, and they can make the angriest person laugh. That magic within their spirit cannot be destroyed by physical death. Although an eyebrow may be slightly raised when you tell someone you saw your deceased mom in detail in a dream, there is great hesitancy in telling others that you heard the whinny of your horse, saw the paw prints of your cat on your comforter, or felt the nudge on your pant leg of your pup, all of which had since passed away. What you experience, though, is what you experience and you don't need validation to make it any more real than what you saw, heard, felt, sensed, or know.

Often we receive a spiritual connection with our passed pets, but we dismiss them as pure coincidences. Sometimes it is the shock of the grief itself that creates a blockage to them. Let me tell you that there are no coincidences, though, only synchronicities, and the more often you allow yourself to believe, the more signs you receive. It doesn't mean that it makes the hurt go away or that you don't miss. Love is deep rooted in this life to the afterlife.

After I said my good-bye to Guinness, I wondered if the journey was worth the pain. I knew that it was, but the sadness created a chasm of uncertainty. I decided that it was. He filled an emptiness that I had. He saved me from myself more times than I could count, and it was my time to let him go and have his Heaven. I knew I'd meet up with him again.

Whether you are grieving a goldfish or a hedgehog, a dog or a cat, horse or a rooster, our pets are cared for, loved, and played with in the afterlife by human souls connected to their human counterparts. They visit their humans, checking up on them and surrounding them with the same unconditional love they did when they were in the physical. Just as human souls heal, relax, and play on the Other Side, so do our pets. When it is their human's time to meet them on the Other Side, they are right there to welcome them just as they did before in life.

Appendix A:
The Transition
to the Other Side

The transition to the Other Side is often an emotional journey for all parties. Sometimes it happens naturally; other times your pet needs some help. Although the transition isn't as much for your pet as it is for you so that you can find your way through the grief.

Create a Space

If you are taking your pet to the vet, or the vet is able to come to you, create a calming space for you all. When we took Guinness to the vet for his final journey, I made sure to gather his favorite blanket and toys, surrounding him with the things that made him feel comfortable. You may also want to put on some soothing and calming music, which can help both you and your pet.

Love

Talk to your pet, sharing your love. Know that sometimes animals don't want to be touched during their transition. It isn't that they are pushing their love away from you, but they may be in pain or extra sensitive.

INVITE

Invite in your angels and loved ones on the Other Side, asking them to help with the transition and show your pet around.

VISUALIZE

Visualize a glowing ball of golden light wrapping around your pet, healing your pet's soul for the journey.

GIVE PERMISSION

Remind your pet that it is okay for them to go, allowing their release from this world to the next.

STAY CALM

Stay as calm and centered as you can. This helps them to not panic. Obviously there will be strong emotions and you might cry.

HONOR

Whether you choose to have their remains cremated, have their body for burial, or neither, find a means to honor the relationship you had. You may want to have a small memorial service, say a prayer, find a poem, plant flowers, or anything else that speaks to you.

DEALING WITH GRIEF OF A PET

I've found in my fifteen plus years of helping make connections with both people and pets here on Earth and the Other Side, that everyone grieves differently. It was in the 1969 book *On Death and*

Dying by Elisabeth Kübler-Ross that the five stages of death were laid out. She also encouraged hospice care, believing that it helped prevent an unsettled spirit and sped up their ability to cross over. It is rare for an animal to have an unsettled spirit, but we certainly often do, even in our grief. We beat ourselves up not grieving enough or grieving too much, or we wonder if we are grieving for the wrong reasons. We wonder if we did the right thing, said the right thing, or if it was interpreted as the right thing. We complicate life from birth to our death, which is why I think we have such a fond love for the simplicity that animals bring us.

Rarely do the stages of grief follow an order, like a flow chart. One minute you will be in denial, then next acceptance, and then bargaining, and then back to denial. Grief is the hardest work you'll ever do.

Denial

Denial can be confusing and comforting. This is when you often recognize the depth of your love and the depth of your loss. You might come home expecting to find your pet, only to remember.

Anger

Although you may be the most rational and pragmatic person, this stage is often filled with unfounded blame and misdirected emotion. You may be upset with the veterinarian, wonder if you should've gotten another opinion, or wonder why you didn't see the illness sooner. You may beat yourself up for not spending enough time with your pet or be angry at a higher power for taking your pet away. And you might even be angry at your pet for leaving you.

Bargaining

This stage could be referred to as the "if only" stage. It's when you feel the need to hit rewind in your mind and wonder what you might've done differently. You might even wonder if you could still do something to help bring your pet back, knowing all the while that isn't a possibility.

Depression

This is when grief becomes real. It's when the deep sadness hits at the reality of the situation. If you feel as if you aren't coming out of this stage, or you keep circling back to this stage, you may want to speak to your physician or a therapist who can offer assistance.

Acceptance

This stage of grief doesn't mean that you forget, but it does mean that you begin to forgive and move forward. You understand that your pet isn't coming back in the physical way, but with acceptance it begins to open up opportunities to experience signs from the Other Side.

DO AND DO NOTS

Most people have good intentions, but so often it can be damaging. The goal of sympathy is to help heal, not hurt. I heard all kinds of horrible things after Guinness passed, from "it's only a dog" to "at least you can still see him." The people saying this might not have realized how hurtful it was, and I think it's because we are often confused as to how to handle a passing, whether it's our own, a family member's, or a friend's.

With as many hurtful comments as I received, I received more lovely ones. It was the ones that helped me celebrate his life and gave me ideas on how to memorialize his spirit that helped me with the grief. I received amazing gifs of candles, photos of Guinness taken from my website, flowers that I planted in my garden in his memory, and even a garden stone with his name on it. It wasn't the physical gifts that helped, it was the love behind them.

WHAT TO DO FOR SOMEONE GRIEVING THEIR PET

- Let them talk when they are ready to talk.
- Listen more than talk, even if there's silence and tears.
- Share a funny or sweet memory about their pet.
- Don't refer to the pet as simply as a dog or a cat, but by their name.
- Be there with a hug.
- Show up with ice cream and a shoulder to cry on.
- Don't give up on them. You might not hear from them for a while, but don't write off their friendship because of this. They have to have time.
- Relay that you will be there for them.
- Help celebrate the life of their pet.
- Suggest they journal.
- Suggest a memorial for their pet (a necklace with their pet's fur in it or a garden stone with the paw print on it).
- Send a card.
- Send flowers and/or call/text.
- Let them know you are thinking of them.
- Send a donation in the deceased pet's name to an organization that benefits animals.

- Offer information on pet loss support groups (there are several).
- If you notice that their grief is deep and possibly suicidal, refer them to professional help, with love.

WHAT NOT TO SAY TO SOMEONE GRIEVING THEIR PET

- *"He/She is in a better place."*—This may be true, but in the mind of a griever the better place is with them.
- *"Just go to the shelter and get another one."*—You don't tell a parent to just pick out another child. Although it might benefit them to get another pet, the timing of that is personal and their choice.
- *"I know how you're feeling."*—Even if you think you do, you really don't.
- *"I don't know what I'd do if I lost my pet."*—They don't either right now, but don't remind them of what you have and they don't.
- *"You'll feel better."*—To them this sounds like "get over it." Mourning isn't like a cold that goes away; it stays with you until you meet your loved ones on the Other Side.
- *"Think of how much more you can do now."*—The more of what they are doing is grieving. Although their time, energy, and money may in fact be freed up without having the pet there, they are only thinking of their loss, not that their trip to Vegas can happen and they don't need a pet sitter.
- *"I never even liked him/her."*—Be nice. You might not have liked their pet. They might have even complained about their pet, but this is not helpful or healing.

- *"How are you doing?"*—They aren't doing. They are grieving and more than likely you will receive an answer that isn't the truth to just make you feel better.
- *"Is there anything I can do?"*—You can't bring their pet back and at this point this is all they want. Instead, just DO something for them.

Other things not to say or do:
- "It's just an animal."
- "It was really old."
- "It was sick."
- "All time heals wounds."
- "Think of the good times."
- "Be grateful for the time you had."
- Don't compare your grief with theirs, or your pet's death with their pet's death.
- Don't tell them for how long they should be sad for or impose a grief timeline.
- Don't bring them another pet.
- Don't tell them to get another pet.
- Don't tell them "it's a blessing."
- Don't tell them "At least they didn't suffer," or, "At least it was a quick death."

Appendix B:
Signs from Your Pet
on the Other Side

Just as our human loved ones on the Other Side give us signs, so do our pets, and they are often in a very similar way. Often your pet will come to you in spirit form to comfort you, and you may experience uncanny signs from a pet from the Other Side. It can come in familiar noises like their snoring, purring, or jingling collar. You might have a dream with them in it or hear someone call out your pet's name. You might even feel them jump on your bed or feel them crawl into your lap. Are you noticing your Heaven hellos?

You Have a Feeling

You might sense you are being watched, have goosebumps for no reason, or simply experience a shiver.

You See

You may see a shadow out of the corner of your eye. You might even find their fur/hair well after you've already cleaned and vacuumed.

Or you may see an indentation of their body on the blanket. You might awake from your sleep to see them standing there, only to disappear. Or you might see another animal that looks exactly like yours.

YOU HEAR

You might hear them whine, bark, meow, or scuffle around. You might hear a bell or a chime of their dog tag.

YOU MAY SMELL

You may smell their scent.

THEY PLAY YOU MUSIC

If there is a song that makes you feel connected to them, you may hear it at unusual times and unusual places.

YOU MIGHT FEEL

You might feel their wet nose against you or feel that they rub up on your leg.

THEY VISIT IN DREAMS

You have a dream about them that feels real and is vivid. The visit will depict them well and happy, even though you may awake and feel sad, missing them all over again.

THEY VISIT THROUGH OTHERS

Someone that you don't know well may bring up information about their pet or tell a story very similar to your experience. Or you may see an animal that reminds you of yours on the Other Side. Pay attention to the people and animals being sent into your life. Pay attention to those that you meet. Maybe you keep meeting someone who has a pet the same name as yours.

THEY SHOW US

They show us numbers, signs, symbols, or license plates. There are no coincidences in life, so if you continue to see the same sequence of numbers come up, a feather continues to fall in front of you, or you keep finding pennies in unusual places make certain to recognize it. It is then that you will receive even more signs.

YOU FIND

You might see a toy that they had at the store or a feather drops from nowhere. You might find a coin in an unusual spot.

YOU MIGHT THINK

You might be going about your day and all of a sudden think of them.

ELECTRONICS

You have electronic disturbances such as a light bulb that keeps burning out or a cell phone that can't keep a charge.

NATURE

They send us signs through nature, like the dragonfly that lands on your shoulder and stays for a bit or the rabbit that your dog always chased around the yard decides to sit on your porch every morning.

There will always be a connection between you and your pets. We often receive these Heaven winks when we most need them, but are so often stressed out that we miss them. What may seem like mere coincidences because more than likely you are getting love from the Other Side.

SIGNS FROM ANIMAL GUIDES

We all have an animal guide, sometimes called power animals or animal totems, whether we know it or don't know it, whether we want it or not. Oftentimes an animal guide isn't a pet that you had in this lifetime, however it can be, as there's no hard and fast rules with regards to this. They show themselves to us through different means, and we often ignore it or disregard it as a coincidence. Yet it is through our animal guides that we receive our spiritual lessons and messages. When doing your pet connection meditation, you may come across another animal that you don't recognize or are surprised showed up.

Our animal guide acts as our teammate, helping us along our confusing path. They often offer signs, but even if we pick up their presence, there's often confusion as to what the sign means. Animal guides can be anything from a domesticated cat to a dolphin. The creature will, however, always be friendly, and is there to help you on your spiritual journey.

Jade could never understand why she loved cows. Since she was a little girl she wanted to wear clothes that depicted a cow, she wanted to decorate her space with pictures of cows, and on the weekends she loved to visit the local dairy farm. It didn't mean she was destined to be a farmer or to own her own cow, but spiritually cows represent fertility and motherly nurturing. Without even understanding the message of her love for cows, Jade became a labor and delivery nurse.

Your animal guide often represents qualities and attributes that you may see in yourself or need to channel to help you with future endeavors. You may have a love for wolves, bears, penguins, otters, gators, or even a unicorn. The attributes of these animals help you to define your balance and find your path.

Often when you do your meditation to connect to your pet on the Other Side, you may meet your animal guide as well. It is this animal guide that can help bridge any gaps you might have in the connection.

Meditation to Connect to Your Pet

Whether you want to connect to your animal guide or your pet on the Other Side, you must first realize that they aren't in a specific place or far away from you, but with and near you, in your heart and always there.

You can lay down in bed or find a comfortable place. Take some deep breaths. Make certain you have enough time to enjoy the meditation. If you have to get up for work or have dinner reservations with friends, you will be clock watching. It is when you can disconnect yourself from the world and empty your mind of the day, when you can connect to the Other Side.

Allow your muscles to relax from your head all the way down to your toes, envisioning a soft white light bathing you in love and relaxation. You can even imagine that white light as a soft and gentle blanket, warming you with love and calmness. Whenever you put it around you, your muscles loosen and your mind quiets.

Some people like to hold a photo of their pet or something that reminds them of the animal. Take a moment to daydream. See their face. Feel their presence. Just let it come, don't chase it. You may feel like you are imagining it at first, and it might take several times for it to feel natural.

Mistrust and lack of patience are the two things that seem to create a blockage on your part. Grief is a barrier as well, but love is even stronger.

Now set your intention and ask for the pet or pets you wish to connect with. Invite them in. Ask that you are protected from all negativity and that only messages which are of the higher good are shared. Ask that the messages are clear.

In your mind's eye, picture a doorway and when you feel comfortable, open the door where you will find yourself standing in the most enchanting place. Tall trees stand proud filled with wisdom and protection. Flowers dot the meadows, colored in hues brighter than you've ever seen. A soft wind wisps around you, comforting and calming you as you make this journey to meet with your pet.

You can feel the sun's rays warming you as you begin your walk along the pathway, taking in all the sights and sounds. With each step, you feel at peace and refreshed. As you turn the corner, you see your pet running toward you. They may have others with them, or they may be alone. You might see them in the physical, feel them, hear them, or just know that they are there. (Be careful to not get frustrated or, if you are coming up blank, think that they've abandoned you. That isn't the case at all. Simply open your eyes and try again when you are in a more relaxed state.) Before you know it, your pet is right in front of you. You can embrace them, speak with them, and even hold them. It is now when you can ask for a message from them. Again, you might hear it or just feel it.

Be open to any and all types of messages. Do not get trapped by wishing for a certain message. Clear your mind completely. Open your heart to its love and lessons. There is a nudge that you must return, but you know that you can return any time to continue your visit. Thank all who showed up and send your gratitude for the messages. Walk back along the pathway until you come to your door, and walk through the door. Slowly return by wiggling your hands and toes, taking some deep breaths in and out and opening your eyes.

Sometimes it helps to record the meditation and playing the recording in your own voice.

MAKE THE CONNECTION

There are times when you don't feel the connection and this often brings up insecurities. Did they love you? Are they mad at you? Did you do everything? Do they truly go to the Other Side? Am I missing my connection?

Stress and mourning often blocks our connections, and you sometimes have to keep an open mind and not get frustrated. Time may not make you forget, but it can help with healing and opening up your connection to the Other Side.

Schedule

Your pets were routine creatures. They knew when you fed them, when you left for work, when you came home from work, and when bedtime was. Schedule time to connect with them on the

Other Side as part of your routine, making sure to give yourself a comfortable space and undisturbed time.

Relax
You don't need to lay on the bed or have a fancy yoga mat. You might be most relaxed in your recliner or even in the bathtub.

Invite
You can ask for their spirit to come out loud or in your head, whatever you feel most comfortable with.

Believe
At first it may seem uncomfortable and unusual, but the more you believe that you can make the connection, the clearer the connection.

Trust
The messages might not make sense at first, but trust that they are the messages you are supposed to hear. You may not understand everything right away.

Don't Expect
Don't expect what you'll hear, sense, see, or feel. Instead allow the messages to just come and simply listen with a clear mind.

Express Gratitude
Even if you didn't have an experience, thank spirit for their help.

Practice
As with anything, the more you practice the easier and clearer the connection will be.

Ask for Help

There are many animal communicators who are gifted and can help you with your connection.

WHAT MIGHT BLOCK YOUR CONNECTION

- Sleep deprivation
- Sleeping aids
- Deep grief
- Alcohol
- Drugs
- Stress

WHAT MIGHT HELP YOU GET CONNECTION

- Healthy eating
- Water
- Exercise
- Routine sleeping patterns
- Consciously being alert
- Journaling
- Ask
- Set up a specific time to make your connection

Bibliography

Barrett, Sir William. *Deathbed Visions*. United Kingdom: White Crow Books, 2011.

Battista, Francis. "The forgotten victims of disaster." CNN.com. August 28, 2015. http://www.cnn.com/2015/08/28/opinions/battista-animals-katrina-aftermath/index.html.

Boltz, Martha M. "Man Chronicles Old Civil War Horse's Life." *Washington Times*, February 6, 2009. http://www.washington times.com/blog/civil-war/2009/feb/6/man-chronicles-old-civil-war-horses-life/.

Chaban, Michele. *The Life Work of Dr. Elisabeth Kübler-Ross and Its Impact on the Death Awareness Movement*. Lewiston, NY: E. Mellen Press, 2000.

Gage, Joan. "Reagan's True White House Ghost Story." Huffington Post. October 13, 2013. http://www.huffingtonpost.com/joan-gage/white-house-ghosts_b_8432426.html.

Gill, Derek. *Quest: The Life of Elisabeth Kübler-Ross*. New York: Ballantine Books, 1982.

Grant, E. K. *Unseen, Unheard, Unspoken: Exploring the Relationship Between Aboriginal Spirituality & Community Development.* Thesis, University of South Australia. 2004.

Grieves, V. *Aboriginal Spirituality: Aboriginal Philosophy, The Basis of Aboriginal Social and Emotional Wellbeing, Discussion Paper No. 9,* Cooperative Research Centre for Aboriginal Health, Darwin. 2009.

Hamilton-Parker, Craig. *What To Do When You Are Dead.* New York: Sterling Imprint, 2010.

"Hurricane Katrina." Louisiana SPCA. Accessed September 2017. http://www.la-spca.org/katrina.

Kelleher, Colm A., and George Knapp. *Hunt for the Skinwalker: Science Confronts the Unexplained at a Remote Ranch.* New York: Paraview Pocket Books, 2005.

Lippy, John D., Jr., *The War Dog.* Harrisburg, PA: The Telegraph Press, 1962.

Nickell, Joe (April 2004). *The Mystery Chronicles: More Real-Life X-Files Hardcover.* Lexington, KY: The University Press of Kentucky, 2010.

Pisa, Nick. "Loyal Dog Attends Mass." Daily Mail Online. January 2013. http://www.dailymail.co.uk/news/article -2263390/Loyal-dog-attends-mass-day-church-owners- funeral-held.html.

Robinett, Kristy. *Higher Intuitions Oracle.* Atglen, PA: Schiffer Publishing, 2013.

Stouffer, Cindy, and Cubbison, Shirley. *A Colonel, a Flag, and a Dog.* Gettysburg, PA: Thomas Publications, 1998.

Worth, Richard. *Elisabeth Kubler-Ross: Encountering Death and Dying*. New York: Facts On File, 2004.

Yonan, Joe. "The death of a pet can hurt as much as the loss of a relative." *The Washington Post*. March 26, 2012. https://www.washingtonpost.com/national/health-science/the-death-of-a-pet-can-hurt-as-much-as-the-loss-of-a-relative/2012/02/21/gIQALXTXcS_story.html?utm_term=.012926f57425.

© E. C. Campbell Photography

ABOUT THE AUTHOR

Kristy Robinett is a psychic medium and author from Michigan who began seeing spirits at the age of three. When she was eight, the spirit of her deceased grandfather helped her escape from a would-be kidnapper, and it was then that Robinett realized the Other Side wasn't so far away. As an adult, she was often called upon by the local police department to examine cold cases in a new light and from a different angle. She gained a solid reputation for being extremely accurate at psychical profiling and giving new perspectives on unsolved crimes. It was then that she began working with a variety of law enforcement agencies, attorneys and private investigators around the United States, aiding in missing persons, arson, and cold cases and in 2014 appeared on a one-hour special on the Investigation Network (ID) called Restless Souls, spotlighting a police case she assisted on.

Robinett teaches psychic development and paranormal investigating at local colleges, lectures across the country and is a regular media commentator. She is the author of *Messages from a Wonderful Afterlife: Signs Loved Ones Send from Beyond, It's a Wonderful Afterlife*; *Forevermore: Guided in Spirit by Edgar Allan Poe*; *Messenger Between Worlds: True Stories from a Psychic Medium*; *Higher Intuitions Oracle*; *Ghosts of Southeast Michigan*; and *Michigan's Haunted Legends and Lore*.

Kristy Robinett is a wife and mom to four adult children and several animals. She enjoys gardening, cooking, exploring old country towns, porch sitting, and graveyards. In 2016, her and her husband bought their dream farmhouse in rural Michigan.

You can visit her online at KristyRobinett.com, facebook.com/kristyrobinett, or Twitter.com/kristyrobinett.

GET MORE AT LLEWELLYN.COM

Visit us online to browse hundreds of our books and decks, plus sign up to receive our e-newsletters and exclusive online offers.

- • Free tarot readings • Spell-a-Day • Moon phases
- • Recipes, spells, and tips • Blogs • Encyclopedia
- • Author interviews, articles, and upcoming events

GET SOCIAL WITH LLEWELLYN

Find us on   @LlewellynBooks

www.Facebook.com/LlewellynBooks

GET BOOKS AT LLEWELLYN

LLEWELLYN ORDERING INFORMATION

Order online: Visit our website at www.llewellyn.com to select your books and place an order on our secure server.

Order by phone:
- • Call toll free within the US at 1-877-NEW-WRLD (1-877-639-9753)
- • We accept VISA, MasterCard, American Express, and Discover.
- • Canadian customers must use credit cards.

Order by mail:
Send the full price of your order (MN residents add 6.875% sales tax) in US funds plus postage and handling to: Llewellyn Worldwide, 2143 Wooddale Drive, Woodbury, MN 55125-2989

POSTAGE AND HANDLING

STANDARD (US):
(Please allow 12 business days)
$30.00 and under, add $6.00.
$30.01 and over, FREE SHIPPING.

INTERNATIONAL ORDERS,
INCLUDING CANADA:
$16.00 for one book, plus $3.00 for each additional book.

Visit us online for more shipping options. Prices subject to change.

FREE CATALOG!

To order, call
1-877-
NEW-WRLD
ext. 8236
or visit our
website

Messenger
between
Worlds

True Stories from a Psychic Medium

Kristy Robinett

Messenger Between Worlds
True Stories from a Psychic Medium
Kristy Robinett

Since the age of three, spirits have come to me in the dead of night, telling me of their woes. Kristy Robinett shares the dramatic, touching, and terrifying moments from her extraordinary life as a psychic medium.

This captivating, powerful memoir is filled with unforgettable scenes: spot-on predictions, countless spirit visits at home and school, menacing paranormal activity, rescue from abduction thanks to her loving grandfather in spirit, and Kristy's first meeting with two spirit guides who become her constant allies. Follow her emotional journey though a difficult childhood, stormy marriages, conflict with faith, job loss, and illness—and the hard-won lessons that opened her heart to true love and acceptance of her unique gift.

978-0-7387-3666-2, 288 pp., 5 ³⁄₁₆ x 8   **$14.99**

forevermore

GUIDED IN SPIRIT BY
EDGAR ALLAN POE

Kristy Robinett

Forevermore
Guided in Spirit by Edgar Allan Poe
Kristy Robinett

Kristy Robinett has always had helpers in spirit, but when she was thirteen, she met the most fascinating spirit guide of all—Edgar Allan Poe. *Forevermore* tells the true story of how Edgar Allan Poe helps Kristy heal her soul so that she is able to fulfill her destiny.

Always reluctant to be known as a psychic, Robinett is shocked when Poe begins helping her discover information about her past lives. Not only does he encourage her to become a writer, but he also teaches her about his life so she is able to help him in his journey as a spirit guide, affirming the comforting fact that we are all given the chance to learn and grow on the other side.

978-0-7387-4067-6, 240 pp., 5 ³⁄₁₆ x 8   **$15.99**

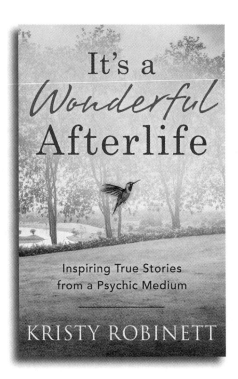

It's a
Wonderful
Afterlife

Inspiring True Stories
from a Psychic Medium

KRISTY ROBINETT

It's a Wonderful Afterlife
Inspiring True Stories from a Psychic Medium
Kristy Robinett

Ever since she was a child, psychic medium Kristy Robinett has communicated with spirits who have shared their experiences of death and what happens afterwards. In this collection of heart-warming stories that answer the most common questions about the afterlife, Robinett delves into the nature of heaven, if there is a hell, and what the transition to the Other Side is like. With personal experiences and stories from clients, Kristy explores the many signs and symbols that our loved ones share with us to assure that it is, indeed, a wonderful afterlife.

978-0-7387-4073-7, 240 pp., 5 ³⁄₁₆ x 8   **$15.99**

Messages
from a
Wonderful
Afterlife

Signs
Loved Ones
Send from Beyond

KRISTY ROBINETT

Author of *It's a Wonderful Afterlife*

Messages From a Wonderful Afterlife
Signs Loved Ones Send from Beyond
Kristy Robinett

Expanding on her previous book, *It's a Wonderful Afterlife*, psychic medium Kristy Robinett shares more personal experiences and stories from clients of how our loved ones—including treasured pets—are communicating from the other side. This heartwarming book teaches you how to identify "heaven hellos" from those in the afterlife and interpret the different signs and symbols that often appear, such as:

Finding coins or feathers · Feeling an invisible touch or shiver down your spine · Seeing a shadow out of the corner of your eye · Smelling a familiar scent · Hearing your deceased loved one's voice · Being visited by a special animal or insect

Messages from a Wonderful Afterlife also provides advice on taking care of yourself while you're grieving and supporting others through times of hardship. With Kristy's guidance, you'll become more aware of your loved ones in spirit and be assured that they're always with you.

978-0-7387-5091-0, 240 pp., 5¼ x 8   **$15.99**

ANIMAL
LESSONS

Discovering Your
Spiritual Connection with Animals

DANIELLE MacKINNON

Animal Lessons
Discovering Your Spiritual Connection with Animals
Danielle MacKinnon

Develop a deeper, more positive relationship with the animals in your life and become a better person using *Animal Lessons*. All around you, animals are acting as therapists, trainers, mentors, and gurus—if you pay attention. They want to guide you toward the next step in your personal evolution, and this first-of-its-kind book shows you how to understand and benefit from them.

Having worked deeply and intuitively with animals for nearly twenty years, Danielle MacKinnon has a wealth of wisdom that she shares through helpful tools and techniques, client stories, and her step-by-step process for personal growth through animal guidance. With an open heart and mind, you'll develop a new awareness and stronger love of yourself as well as the wise creatures in your life.

978-0-7387-5135-1, 240 pp., 5¼ x 8   **$15.99**

Identify, Attune, and Connect to the
Energy of Animals

Animal
Frequency

Melissa Alvarez

A REFERENCE TO 200 WILD, DOMESTIC,
AND MYTHICAL CREATURES

Animal Frequency
Identify, Attune, and Connect to the Energy of Animals
MELISSA ALVAREZ

Discover the energetic power of animals and how to connect with their frequencies in order to grow spiritually. This easy-to-use, A to Z reference guide contains encyclopedic listings for nearly two hundred animals—wild, domestic, and mythical—and easy techniques and visualizations for building relationships with them, including energetically bonding with your pets. All animals possess a distinctive energy vibration that can connect with yours, allowing you to communicate with them and understand their role in your spiritual development.

978-0-7387-4928-0, 432 pp., 7½ x 9¼   **$24.99**
